INSTITUTE OF PACIFIC RELATIONS

INQUIRY SERIES

The Institute of Pacific Relations is an unofficial and non-political body, founded in 1925 to facilitate the scientific study of the peoples of the Pacific Area. It is composed of National Councils in eleven countries.

The Institute as such and the National Councils of which it is composed are precluded from expressing an opinion on any aspect of national or international affairs; opinions expressed in this study are, therefore, purely individual.

BRITISH FAR EASTERN POLICY

BRITISH FAR EASTERN POLICY

By

G. E. HUBBARD

Far Eastern Research Secretary,
Royal Institute of International Affairs

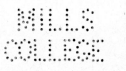

I. P. R. INQUIRY SERIES

INTERNATIONAL SECRETARIAT

INSTITUTE OF PACIFIC RELATIONS

PUBLICATIONS OFFICE, 129 EAST 52ND STREET, NEW YORK

1943

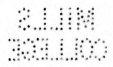

FOREWORD

This study forms part of the documentation of an Inquiry organized by the Institute of Pacific Relations into the problems arising from the conflict in the Far East.

It has been prepared by Mr. G. E. Hubbard, Far Eastern Research Secretary, Royal Institute of International Affairs; author of *Eastern Industrialization and Its Effect on the West*. This study is a revision and enlargement of an earlier pamphlet published under the same title by the Royal Institute of International Affairs. Chapters I to IV of this revised version were submitted in mimeographed form as a document for the Mont Tremblant Conference of the I.P.R., December 1942; Chapter V was added in April 1943.

The Study has been submitted in draft to a number of authorities, many of whom made suggestions and criticisms which were of great value in the process of revision.

Though many of the comments received have been incorporated in the final text, the above authorities do not of course accept responsibility for the study. The statements of fact or of opinion appearing herein do not represent the views of the Institute of Pacific Relations or of the Pacific Council or of any of the National Councils. Such statements are made on the sole responsibility of the author.

During 1938 the Inquiry was carried on under the general direction of Dr. J. W. Dafoe as Chairman of the Pacific Council and since 1939 under his successors Dr. Philip C. Jessup and Mr. Edgar J. Tarr. Every member of the International Secretariat has contributed to the research and editorial work in connection with the Inquiry, but special mention should be made of Mr. W. L. Holland, Miss Kate Mitchell and Miss Hilda Austern, who have carried the major share of this responsibility.

In the general conduct of this Inquiry into the problems arising from the conflict in the Far East the Institute has benefited by the counsel of the following Advisers:

Professor H. F. Angus of the University of British Columbia.

Dr. J. B. Condliffe of the University of California

M. Etienne Dennery of the Ecole des Sciences Politiques.

These Advisers have co-operated with the Chairman and the Secretary-General in an effort to insure that the publications issued in connection with the Inquiry conform to a proper standard of sound and impartial scholarship. Each manuscript has been submitted to

vii

at least two of the Advisers and although they do not necessarily subscribe to the statements or views in this or any of the studies, they consider this study to be a useful contribution to the subject of the Inquiry.

The purpose of this Inquiry is to relate unofficial scholarship to the problems arising from the present situation in the Far East. Its purpose is to provide members of the Institute in all countries and the members of I.P.R Conferences with an impartial and constructive analysis of the situation in the Far East with a view to indicating the major issues, which must be considered in any future adjustment of international relations in that area. To this end, the analysis will include an account of the economic and political conditions which produced the situation existing in July 1937, with respect to China, to Japan and to the other foreign Powers concerned; an evaluation of developments during the war period which appear to indicate important trends in the policies and programs of all the Powers in relation to the Far Eastern situation; and finally, an estimate of the principal political, economic and social conditions which may be expected in a post-war period, the possible forms of adjustment which might be applied under these conditions, and the effects of such adjustments upon the countries concerned.

The Inquiry does not propose to "document" a specific plan for dealing with the Far Eastern situation. Its aim is to focus available information on the present crisis in forms which will be useful to those who lack either the time or the expert knowledge to study the vast amount of material now appearing or already published in a number of languages.

The present study, "British Far Eastern Policy," falls within the framework of the first of the four general groups of studies which it is proposed to make as follows:

I. The political and economic conditions which have contributed to the present course of the policies of Western Powers in the Far East; their territorial and economic interests; the effects on their Far Eastern policies of internal economic and political develoments and of developments in their foreign policies vis-à-vis other parts of the world; the probable effects of the present conflict on their positions in the Far East; their changing attitudes and policies with respect to their future relations in that area.

II. The political and economic conditions which have contributed to the present course of Japanese foreign policy and possible important future developments; the extent to which Japan's policy toward China has been influenced by Japan's geographic conditions and material resources, by special features in the political and economic organization of Japan which directly or indirectly affect the formulation of her present foreign policy, by economic and political developments in China, by the external policies of other Powers affecting Japan; the principal political, economic and social factors which may be expected in a post-war Japan; possible and probable adjustments on the part of other nations which could aid in the solution of Japan's fundamental problems.

III. The political and economic conditions which have contributed to the present course of Chinese foreign policy and possible important future developments; Chinese unification and reconstruction, 1931-37, and steps leading toward the policy of united national resistance to Japan; the present degree of political cohesion and economic strength; effects of resistance and current developments on the position of foreign interests in China and changes in China's relations with foreign Powers; the principal political, economic and social factors which may be expected in a post-war China; possible and probable adjustments on the part of other nations which could aid in the solution of China's fundamental problems.

IV. Possible methods for the adjustment of specific problems, in the light of information and suggestions presented in the three studies outlined above; analysis of previous attempts at bilateral or multilateral adjustments of political and economic relations in the Pacific and causes of their success or failure; types of administrative procedures and controls already tried out and their relative effectiveness; the major issues likely to require international adjustment in a post-war period and the most helpful methods which might be devised to meet them; necessary adjustments by the Powers concerned; the basic requirements of a practical system of international organization which could promote the security and peaceful development of the countries of the Pacific area.

EDWARD C. CARTER
Secretary-General

New York,
June 15, 1943

TABLE OF CONTENTS

BRITISH FAR EASTERN POLICY

CHAPTER I

INTRODUCTION

The broad trends of a country's foreign policy are, in the final analysis, the reflection of its national interests in the most fundamental sense, and need to be set against these as a background in order to be rightly understood.

A study of Great Britain's Far Eastern policy may, therefore, be introduced by defining as succinctly as possible the basic interests of the British people.[1] Reduced to four main essentials,[2] they are:

1. Livelihood—the safeguarding of British standards of life against excessive deterioration.

2. Security—safety from hostile action against British territorial possessions and essential lines of communication, and the power to defeat such action if it should eventuate.

3. Peace—preservation from the evils of war in the widest sense.

4. Political Liberty—the retention of the power to exercise freely British conceptions of liberty in the face of danger of submergence by antagonistic "ideologies."[3]

From these four basic British interests there have evolved certain maxims of British foreign policy, both general and in relation to the Far East in particular.

[1] The meaning attachable to the epithet *British* in a study of British policy must depend in some degree upon the emphasis to be laid on United Kingdom viewpoints as compared with British Commonwealth viewpoints. The present study has been made primarily from the United Kingdom viewpoint, since this was required for the purposes of the Institute of Pacific Relations, which comprises national councils in Canada, Australia, and New Zealand among its constituent bodies and relies upon them for the expression of the viewpoints of the individual Dominions.

[2] Set out irrespectively of their order of relative importance.

[3] The inclusion of this fourth "vital interest" on a par with the other three obviously needs no justification in the present state of the world. After the time of the Napoleonic wars the idea of the preservation of liberties being a fundamental British interest had, it is true, become strange to the ordinary Englishman till the War of 1914-18 caused a revival of "ideological" thinking, which became greatly intensified, and more or less universal, after the entry on to the scene of militarily powerful countries with political philosophies opposed on essential points to British democratic and liberal ideas.

From the first mentioned—the conservation of national standards of life—there arose the doctrine of the "Open Door," that is the assurance of a free field for commercial enterprise without privilege or preference for any one country. The reason for this becoming a British maxim of policy is not difficult to perceive. British standards of life have been for well over a century past, indissolubly bound up with Great Britain's role as a universal trader, carrier, banker, and entrepreneur, and her success in this role has depended on ability to secure freedom of commercial opportunity over a major part of the world. The need for this freedom dictated the policy of (a) opening up, and of keeping open, to British enterprise, foreign markets, trade routes, and fields for capital investment, and (b) resisting attempts at "ringfencing" by other nations. Thus the "Open Door" became a corner stone of British foreign policy. In the Far East it attained particular importance on account of the fact that China with her vast population, latent wealth, and economic under-development presented one of the most promising fields for commercial development. She was at the same time particularly susceptible to the danger of partition owing to her relative weakness. As a corollary to the doctrine of the "Open Door" Great Britain, therefore, adopted the doctrine of the maintenance in being of an independent China as the best guarantee against Powers, especially those within striking range of China, acquiring exclusive rights and monopolies detrimental to British commercial enterprise.

For security (the second on the list of basic British interests) Great Britain traditionally relied in the first instance on her own armaments, and, secondly, on the policy of creating a counterpoise to whatever Power, or group of Powers, might threaten her safety by attaining a position of too great military predominance. In the case of the Far East, the first of these props to security required that adequate naval and military measures should be taken for protecting the British possessions in the Pacific, the line of communications to Australia and New Zealand, and the eastern approaches to the Indian Ocean. This was a task which affected domestic, rather than foreign policy. The second prop took the form of a consistent attempt to maintain what became known as "the balance of power." During the phase of "splendid isolation" in the latter part of the 19th century British statesmen counted on preserving a balance of power by intervening, if necessary, in any major dispute on the side of the weaker party. When, at the close of the century, the isolation policy was discarded, the British Government pursued the same goal of a balance of power by means of *ententes* concluded with other great Powers. They still held to the same purpose at the close of the Great War, when Great Britain at first threw her weight on the side of collective security, trusting to this to take the place of bilateral engagements as a means of combining forces to counter aggression by any would-be dominant Power. The "balance of power objective," construed in a wide sense, can thus be added to the constants in British policy, whether considered generally or with special relation to the Far East.

The desire to find means of preserving peace as an end in itself engendered the policy of support for the League of Nations with its principles of the peaceful adjustment of disputes, renunciation of war as an instrument of policy, and limitation of armaments—a policy which, in spite of notable setbacks, was operative in the British handling of Far Eastern affairs from 1919 until the acknowledged breakdown of the collective security system.

No specific British policy can be said to have been evolved for the safeguarding of British concepts of liberty, and, so far at least as Government policy was concerned, there was till shortly before the war an avowed disinclination to participate in anything in the nature of a banding together of democratic against totalitarian nations, or to encourage in any way the dividing up of the world into ideological camps. This phase passed away, however, as war approached, and there was a strong British response to the movement for cooperation between "like-minded" nations in upholding the principles of liberty which they shared.

The essential ingredients of British Far Eastern policy, viewed as part of her general policy up to the beginning of the present war therefore consisted of: (1) the "Open Door," with which was coupled the preservation of an independent China; (2) equilibrium of power; (3) adequate provision for regional defense; (4) regional peace and stability assured by international agreement, and (5) the promotion of collaboration among "like-minded" Powers. To show how these objectives became translated into political action is the main purpose of the following chapters.

It has become increasingly clear that the year 1931 rules a dividing line across the pages of Far Eastern political history. Before the Manchurian Affair the focus was mainly on China. Since then the focus has moved to Japan, whose record of aggressive action in East Asia leads in an unbroken trail from Mukden to Pearl Harbor. For the sake of convenience we may call the two eras the "old," and the "new." In analyzing British Far Eastern policy the question inevitably arises as to what proportion of attention should be given respectively to the "old" and the "new," and as to how far back in the history of the Far East it is desirable and necessary to go.

If at first sight it appears that an undue proportion of space has been given to the "old" era as compared with the "new," there is justification for the line adopted in the following three facts. Firstly, the "old" was the formative period for British Far Eastern policy, and trends which were then evolved have persisted up to the present time, retaining, albeit in a state of latency, much of their original force. Secondly, British "policy," as conceived of in this study, includes both purpose and performance—what the Government aims at and what it does in the field of action. In a period when the two run parallel the examination of diplomatic action over the period in question is in itself an adequate guide to the underlying purpose. But during the "new" era British diplomacy in the Far East has been too much at the mercy of external forces and of refractory local conditions for this to have been the case, and one must go back to earlier periods to see British policy (as understood in the wider sense) manifesting itself in diplomatic action without too much distortion from outside influences. Thirdly, the need for a detailed record of British diplomatic action in the Far East during the "new," i. e., post-1931, period has been met by other publications issued by the Institute of Pacific Relations, in particular in Mr. Irving Friedman's *British Relations with China, 1931-39.*

CHAPTER II

BEFORE THE MANCHURIAN AFFAIR

1. *First Phase: From 1834 to the Sino-Japanese War of 1894-95*

In 1834 the British Government superseded the East India Company in the general management of the British trading community at Canton and in the conduct of relations with the Chinese authorities. For the next sixty years Great Britain was chiefly occupied in the Far East with the development of her commercial interests in China and Japan, particularly the former. It was a phase of British Far Eastern policy which may, in fact, be described as the commercial phase *par excellence*. On the one hand, the wave of British colonial expansion which had washed over India and Africa having died down to a ripple on the edge of the Far East, such slight British ambitions of territorial acquisition as were entertained in respect to that area were merely incidental to the object of developing trade. Sir Frederick Whyte says in *China and Foreign Powers*[1] "trade was ever our first interest . . . we have never willingly passed beyond it to found even the beginnings of an Empire in the East," though this does not mean that British policy in the Far East was altogether exempt from the influence of the imperialistic habits of thought which were current among many of the leading British statesmen of the day. On the other hand the rapid industrialization of Great Britain created an urgent need for fields for commercial expansion, and it became a primary object of British policy to secure a market in a part of the world which appeared to contain greater trading potentialities than any other. China, in particular, figured constantly in British eyes as a commercial *Eldorado* offering limitless prospects to a great manufacturing nation like Great Britain.

The principal task before British diplomacy during the greater part of this period was, therefore, that of progressively opening up the China market, a process which involved the breaking down of Chinese active and passive resistance to

[1] *China and Foreign Powers*, Oxford University Press, 1927, p. 36.

7

foreign penetration. The immediate objective at the start was to induce the Chinese to accept the axiom of "equality" (involving the practice of direct diplomatic intercourse on the part of the Chinese Imperial Government) and the "rule of law" in the treatment of foreign traders in China—two principles essential to the free development of commercial intercourse with any Western nation. These objectives were not achieved without resort to force, and they led to war on three occasions. Although the campaigns which Great Britain launched against China in 1840, 1857, and 1860 would assuredly be condemned by British standards of conscience today, there is clear enough evidence that they were entered into by the responsible English statesmen less in a spirit of "jingoism" (a spirit which it would be vain to deny had in the nineteenth century its periods of influence on British policy in some parts of the world) than in a spirit of revolt against what were genuinely felt to be intolerable grievances. Injustices—as seen through English eyes—were strenuously resisted and the Chinese officials at Canton were placed under strong pressure to relax from their superior attitude towards the foreigner. But there was in those early years no desire, or attempt, to ride roughshod over Chinese authority or native custom. Lord Napier, the first permanent representative of the British Government in China, was in fact given express instructions to "conform to Chinese regulations and to consider Chinese prejudices." Even less than a year before the outbreak of the first Anglo-Chinese war, Lord Palmerston showed in no uncertain language his disapprobation of lawless interference with China's sovereign rights. In a case in which force had been used to resist the Chinese authorities, he indignantly inquired from the Superintendent of Trade at Canton "upon what alleged ground of right these persons considered themselves entitled to interfere with the arrangements made by the Chinese officers of justice."[2] With regard, again, to the levying of taxes on merchandise, the Foreign Secretary took the line that China had the right to impose whatever duties she chose and that "we (the British) cannot claim for British goods treatment not given to Chinese goods,"[3] but he insisted that taxation must be imposed regularly and indiscriminately.

[2] W. C. Costin: *Great Britain and China 1933-1960*, Oxford, 1937, p. 52.
[3] This was, of course, before the conclusion of the first China treaties, whereby foreigners became exempt from many kinds of exaction to which Chinese merchants remained subject.

Thus we come to the much disputed question of the China opium trade, in which Great Britain had the predominant, though by no means exclusive share. It is a question which has received so much prominence from writers on early Anglo-Chinese relations that it seems well to deal with the subject more fully than is strictly required by this study of British Government policy.

It is undeniable that the traffic in opium imported from India to Canton was morally scandalous—and none the less so because the anti-opium laws of China (the importation of opium had been prohibited by an Imperial edict in the year 1800) were habitually disregarded by the Chinese themselves, both merchants and officials, so that the trade flourished openly at Canton, or else were used by the local authorities as a means of extorting illicit gain as the price of connivance at the importation of the drug. On the British side the incentive to indulge in the trade lay partly in the great profits to be gained by the interested parties in India—including the Government, to whom as a monopoly-holder in certain parts of the country the opium revenue was very important—and partly in the value of opium sales in China as a means of redressing the very heavy and embarrassing adverse balance of Great Britain's trade with China. It was this latter consideration which had led the East India Company, while strictly abjuring participation in the trade so long as it was illegal, to do nothing to discourage, but rather to encourage, the "interlopers" whose operations provided a supply of bills of exchange which were invaluable to the Company for financing its export trade from Canton.

We are here primarily concerned, however, with the British Government's position in relation to the opium trade. Whatever tenable ground there is for reprobating their attitude lies in this fact; in upholding, up to the point of force of arms, the principle of "square dealing" they allowed the principle to embrace the technically illegal and morally reprehensible opium traffic, making no distinction between it and other forms of commerce on strictly moral grounds, although they did, as we shall see, discriminate on the ground of its illegality under Chinese law. The attitude which the Government took cannot be described better than in Lord Palmerston's own words, and the following three quotations from his dispatches will serve to show quite clearly how the Government approached this vexed question.[4]

"Her Majesty's Government," Lord Palmerston wrote in a letter to Captain Elliot, "by no means dispute the right of the Government of China to prohibit the importation of opium into China, and to seize and confiscate any opium which, in defiance of prohibition duly made, should be brought by foreigners or Chinese subjects into the territories of the Empire. But these fiscal prohibitions ought to be impartially and steadily enforced."

With reference to the protection to be given to British opium smugglers Lord Palmerston's instructions to Captain Elliot were as follows:[5]

"Her Majesty's Government cannot interfere for the purpose of enabling British subjects to violate the laws of the country to which they trade. Any loss, therefore, which such persons may suffer in consequence of the more effectual execution of the Chinese laws on this subject, must be borne by the parties who have brought that loss on themselves by their own acts."

Finally, in February 1840, when the Chinese High Commissioner at Canton had secured the surrender of 20,000 chests of British-owned opium, and had demanded *inter alia* that ships and cargoes should be liable in the future to seizure and confiscation and that foreigners involved should be surrendered for trial and execution, and when the refusal of these demands had been followed by the withdrawal of all the British merchants from Canton and the suspension of British trade with the port, Lord Palmerston squarely set out the British Government's position in the following terms:[6]

"It appears that the Laws of the Chinese Empire forbid the importation of opium into China, and declare that all opium which may be brought into the country is liable to confiscation.

"The Queen of England desires that Her subjects who may go into Foreign Countries should obey the laws of those countries and Her Majesty does not wish to protect them from the just consequences of any offences which they may commit in foreign ports. But, on the other hand, Her Majesty cannot permit that Her subjects residing abroad should be treated with violence, and be exposed to insult and injustice; and when wrong is done to them, Her Majesty will see that they obtain redress.

"Now if a Government makes a Law which applies both to its own

[4] Costin: *op. cit.*, p. 60.
[5] *Ibid.*, pp. 47-8.
[6] Public Record Office: F.O. 17/37.

subjects and to Foreigners, such Government ought to enforce that Law impartially or not at all. If it enforces that Law on Foreigners, it is bound to enforce it also upon its own subjects, and it has no right to permit its own subjects to violate the law with impunity, and then to punish Foreigners for doing the very same thing.

"Neither is it just that such a law should for a great length of time be allowed to sleep as a dead letter, and that both natives and foreigners should be taught to consider it as of no effect, and that then suddenly, and without sufficient warning, it should be put in force with the utmost vigour and severity.

"Now although the Law of China declares that the importation of opium should be forbidden, yet it is notorious that for many years past, that importation has been connived at, and permitted by the Chinese authorities at Canton, nay, more, that those authorities, from the Governor downwards, have made an annual and considerable profit by taking money from Foreigners for the permission to import opium; and of late the Chinese authorities have gone so far in setting this law at defiance that Mandarin Boats were employed to bring opium to Canton from the Foreign ships lying at Lintin."

In the light of these statements of the British Government's attitude by its most authoritative spokesman, it seems impossible to find justification for the often repeated accusation that the Anglo-Chinese wars were fought by Great Britain in order to force opium on China. The opium question was, in point of fact, incidental, and there can be practically no doubt that if no opium ship had ever come to Canton, the wars would still have taken place, since their real object was, as had already been made clear, to put an end to what the British Government saw as intolerable restrictions on the freedom of trade and the liberty of individual traders, and furthermore to impose upon China British standards of international intercourse—in short to "open the door." As was said at the time by John Quincy Adams, at one time American Secretary of State, the real cause of war was not opium but the "kow-tow."

To conclude the story of the opium dispute it should be added that there was no reference to opium in the Nanking Treaty. On the other hand the Chinese anti-opium laws though not repealed were in practice allowed by tacit agreement to remain a dead letter. The opium import trade was eventually legalized and subjected to regular Customs dues by a convention concluded at Shanghai between Lord Elgin and the Chinese Commissioners in 1858. Foreigners were not allowed, however, to transport opium into the interior and the Chinese

Government remained free to impose whatever internal transit dues they liked.

It is open to question whether the legalistic attitude adopted by the British Government justified a resort to arms to impose standards of conduct on an oriental people with totally different traditions. Nor can it be said that, in their handling of the opium question, the British Government reflected adequately that sense of conscience and humanitarian feeling among large classes of Englishmen which had inspired the suppression of the African slave-trade in the teeth of important vested interests. The Opposition in Parliament, in fact, took issue with the Government over the moral aspect of the question, and their leader, Mr. Gladstone, declared that it was "mere mockery" to affect indignation about the pernicious opium trade while refusing to the Chinese Government the right to take every means to crush it, even if such action included indiscriminate action against the entire merchant community at Canton.

Meanwhile the evidence afforded by the instructions given to the British agents on the spot shows the existence of an underlying concern, even in times of intense friction, to maintain in principle the effectiveness of Chinese authority. This was from the start recognized as being a British interest. Even British officials on the spot, who were by their immersion in current problems less able as a rule to take a detached "long-term" view of policy, realized the dangers of undermining the ruling powers in China. Thus Captain Elliot in 1840 deprecated a proposal to send plenipotentiaries to Peking on the ground that, if they were insulted, this might lead on to such retaliatory action as would endanger the ruling dynasty and produce a political convulsion in China, than which, he wrote, "I cannot conceive a more unfortunate consequence to ourselves." Almost from the start a distinction arose between the attitude of the British officials and that of the British merchants towards the question of Chinese jurisdiction. The license claimed, and practised, by many of the merchants was regularly frowned upon by the Home Government and their representatives on the spot, so much so that in a petition addressed to the House of Commons the merchants complained that the British Minister and consular officers showed a positive bias against British subjects. In much the same way at a later date when a British subject was Inspector General of the Chinese Maritime Customs he was accused of weighting the scales against his fellow countrymen—a charge which had at least this much foundation that Sir Robert Hart was scrupulously loyal to the interests of the Government which he served and careful to avoid any favor to British or foreign interests as such.

A competent summing-up of British policy of this early period has been given by Mr. W. C. Costin[7] in the following terms:

"The old colonial policy of the eighteenth century which aimed at isolation and monopoly had given place before the beginning of our story to the new idea of free trade and the principle of the "open door" . . . The pushing and grasping merchant in China . . . seemed indeed to have no time and little inclination for matters of eternal moment . . . But it is a matter worthy of note that the British Government was as deeply conscious of its responsibility as it was of its power. From the beginning it sought to control and govern its unruly subjects. A man like Palmerston was not only steeped in the conception of the Rule of Law, but was by temperament a grand hater of injustice and by instinct a member of a class whose right and duty it was to govern.

"If in his conduct the individual Englishman was sometimes harsh and even brutal, it may be thought that Palmerston was not essentially different when he used his Big Stick of a naval demonstration or a small punitive force. But it would appear that the British Government was unwilling to use that Stick save as an instrument of what it considered justice in a legally ordered international society. It is not difficult for it to plead at the bar of international law that the Stick was not brandished for the sake of mere expediency. Both in the question of the exchange of ports and in the regulation of the opium trade in 1858, two matters which deeply concerned British interests, the Government and its representative were careful not to arrive at their ends by forceful means. When they used force it was to meet the duplicity, evasion, cunning, and cruelty of the Chinese officials."

As the trade of other countries with China developed, Great Britain automatically became more and more the champion of foreign rights and privileges as a whole. The British Government's attitude towards foreign competitors has been well summarized by Mr. T. W. Overlach[8] as follows:

"In accordance with the *laissez-faire* and free-trade principles England was ready after having obtained new outlets for trade and other privileges, to share them with other nations. Thus her acquisition of trade facilities was followed by the conclusion of similar treaties between China and other Powers. Britain had solved the problem of the conditions most favorable to national prosperity in her way, believing that open competition

[7] Costin: *op. cit.*, pp. 343-4.
[8] In *Foreign Financial Control in China*, New York, 1919, p. 21.

was the best condition for ensuring such prosperity. Wherever free trade existed it meant British preponderance; and the predominance of England in China was admitted on all hands. Consequently, Great Britain did not attain exclusive privileges for the benefit of her trade and she strove by means of the 'most favoured nation' clause only to enjoy such privileges as have been accorded to other nations and no more. And she also was willing to refrain from the exaction of further privileges."

The absence of exclusiveness as an aim of British policy was emphasized by the Government itself. For instance, the instructions to Lord Elgin, when he departed on his mission to China in 1856, required him to bear in mind that "Her Majesty's Government have no desire to obtain any exclusive advantages for British trade in China, but are only desirous to share with other nations any benefits which they may acquire in the first instance specifically for British commerce." But at the same time other Western Powers were easing British shoulders of some of the diplomatic burden, for, as Mr. A. J. Sargent[9] points out, after the 1860 war between China and England and France there opened a new phase in which purely individual action by Great Britain began to be superseded by concerted action on the part of the Powers interested in China. The lines of policy pursued by the British Government itself, Mr. Sargent goes on to criticize in the following words: "They contained the old principle of coercion and local pressure and the new plan of negotiation with the Chinese Government; they included points which might readily be conceded by the Chinese and others which could only be satisfied by a revolutionary change in the Chinese character and administration." Their behavior bore evidence, he concluded, that the British Government were still at a loss as to the right method of dealing with an Eastern Power. The Burlinghame Mission of 1868 did indeed do something to give direction to the British Government's course by confirming them in the principle of dealing direct with the Central Government and of abjuring "local pressure." The success of the Mission in London was "less spectacular, but more practical"[10] than its effect in Washington. After his interview with Mr. Burlinghame, Lord Clarendon, who was then Foreign Secretary, made a statement of the British Government's intentions (which were subsequently translated into instructions to the

[9] In *Anglo-Chinese Commerce and Diplomacy*, Oxford, 1907, pp. 109-10.
[10] H. B. Morse and H. F. MacNair: *Far Eastern International Relations*, Commercial Press, Shanghai, 1925, p. 385.

British Minister in Peking), under the following two heads,[11] first "that an unfriendly pressure shall not be applied inconsistent with the independence and safety of China," and secondly "that Her Majesty's Government desires to deal directly with the Central Government rather than with the local authorities," with the reservation that force might be used to protect life and property against any immediate danger.

The expectation of a substantial improvement in the relationships between Great Britain and China was, unfortunately, defeated, on the one hand, by the unreliability of the Manchu Government and the weakness of its hold over the authorities in the provinces, and, on the other hand, by the decline of statesmanship which took place about this time in the conduct of British Far Eastern diplomacy, which under Lord Palmerston's successors lost much of its pristine energy and failed to grapple effectively with the difficulties of an always obscure situation.

Reviewing Great Britain's "open door" policy in the sense in which it can be applied to this first phase of her Far Eastern relations, we may say that it had in practice two aspects—vis-à-vis the oriental countries, it meant the forcing open of channels of trade, vis-à-vis other Western nations, it meant the sharing out of the resulting benefits. When, for instance, Great Britain by the Treaty of Nanking obtained the cession of Hongkong as a trade depot and dockyard for merchant shipping, they had made it open to all, no special privileges being given to British merchants or British vessels; and when, mainly by British action, foreign municipal government was set up at Shanghai, the Municipal Council which resulted was established on an international footing. And so, "in the wake of international readjustment the United States and other (sic) European nations plunged into the field with alacrity and peacefully secured the privileges enjoyed by the British."[12]

This cursory survey of British relations with China in the nineteenth century has provided sufficient illustration of two of the earliest and most permanent features of British Far Eastern policy—the principle of the "open door" and the axiom that Chinese integrity should be preserved. But nothing has

[11] *Ibid.*, p. 386.
[12] P. C. Kuo: *Critical Study of the first Anglo-Chinese War*, Commercial Press, Shanghai, 1935, p. 199.

yet been said about British policy towards Japan, and before passing on to the next phase we must cast an eye over Anglo-Japanese relations during the earlier period.

The general principles which during the nineteenth century governed British policy in China applied also to British policy towards Japan. There also, once the door had been opened to foreign trade, it was the object of the British Government to maintain it on a footing of equal opportunity to all, and—for both commercial and political reasons—to preserve the unity and integrity of the Japanese Empire. This led, as we shall see, to an intimate connection between British diplomacy and internal Japanese politics.

A primarily commercial policy not unnaturally tended to regard Japan, the smaller nation and lesser market, as of subsidiary importance to China, and Great Britain had been content to follow in the footsteps of America in opening the country, so that when Lord Elgin concluded the first comprehensive British treaty of commerce in 1858 as part of his general mission in the Far East, he found the way already prepared for him by the work of Commodore Perry and Mr. Townsend Harris. Although Great Britain thus followed the American lead in the preliminary stages, it was her representatives who gave the first evidence of realizing the growing weakness of the Shogunate, together with the strength of the movement among the Western clans for its abolition and for the restoration of full political authority to the Emperor. This movement was of particular importance because in Japan, as in China, one of the principal problems at the start was to create effective diplomatic contact with the real repository of governing power in the land. Contrary to the policies of certain other Powers, "The British Legation was determined that, so far as their influence went, the Mikado should be restored to the headship of the nation, so that treaties with foreign Powers might receive a sanction that no one would venture to dispute."[13] In 1865 British influence was pre-eminent in securing the Imperial ratification of the treaties whereby the ground was cut from under the feet of the anti-foreign party. British influence again prevented any foreign intervention on the side of the Shogunate during the civil war of 1868-9 and brought about a proclamation of neutrality by

[13] Sir E. Satow: *A Diplomat in Japan,* Seeley Service & Co., Ltd., London, 1921, p. 244.

the Powers, which has been described as having been "without doubt a tremendous help for the Imperial cause."[14]

In the ensuing decades British diplomacy favored the moderate party of peaceful reconstruction in Japan as against the military extremists, who left to themselves, would have rushed into war with Korea and with her suzerain, China. British influence was also exerted to bring about a peaceful composition of the Formosan, Korean and Liuchiu Islands dispute. The motives were similar to those which we shall presently see operating in British relations with China. The British Government feared that Japanese encroachment in Korea would lead to a Sino-Japanese War, which, in turn, would result in the exhaustion of the Asiatic combatants and might be followed by Russian territorial acquisitions at the expense of all three, a consummation which Great Britain was most anxious to avoid.

In thus trying to preserve peace in East Asia and to ensure the political integrity and administrative progress of the three countries China, Japan and Korea, British policy was in line with that of the United States. This fact was unfortunately often obscured in the minds of American diplomatic representatives in the Far East by long-lingering suspicions of British territorial designs upon the countries concerned, and it may well be a subject for conjecture whether, had the objectives of British policy been more correctly appreciated at Washington in 1894, the British proposal for joint intervention to prevent the then impending Sino-Japanese conflict might not have been more sympathetically received, with incalculable effects on subsequent events.

By taking the initiative towards the end of the century in renouncing extra-territorial rights in Japan, the British Government strengthened the ties between the two countries which were to culminate in the next century in a treaty of alliance. Already in 1873 they had declared that they "would see with great satisfaction the establishment in Japan of order and justice as the rule of administration permanently accepted and observed, which would enable them with confidence to entrust the interests of British subjects, as in most countries, to the safekeeping of the local Government." Until they were satisfied that the conditions laid down in 1873 would be fulfilled the

[14] Dr. R. H. Akagi: *Japan's Foreign Relations 1542-1936*, Hokuseido Press, Tokyo, 1936, p. 57.

British Government were, however, averse to the relinquishment of consular jurisdiction (for which there was at that time no precedent) and twenty years elapsed before the final step was taken. The long delay is partly explicable by the fact that the "era of enlightenment" in Japan was meanwhile being menaced by a series of internal crises, such as the Satsuma Rebellion of 1877-8. Even in 1894, there was, as Count Mutsu, then Japanese Foreign Minister, admitted, a substantial Japanese body of opinion which would have preferred to retain the old treaties rather than allow foreigners into the interior. When, therefore, the British Government between 1890 and 1894 assumed the lead in negotiations which led to the eventual abandonment of British extra-territorial rights in the manner provided for in the Anglo-Japanese Treaty of July 16, 1894, they were taking a step in the dark—a step which, however, proved to be justified by the event, and which paved the way to the succeeding era of close Anglo-Japanese cooperation in the affairs of the Far East.

2. *Second Phase: From the Sino-Japanese War of 1894-95 to the Great War of 1914-18*

As time went on there was a widening and a diversification of Great Britain's commercial interest in China. At first this had been confined to actual trade, originally as a source of profit to a close corporation of East India merchants, and later as an outlet for British manufactures and a consequent means of support for the British working population, especially those engaged in textile industries. But as commercial intercourse developed, services ancillary to trade—shipping, banking, insurance, et cetera—grew in importance as part of Britain's commercial "stake" in the Far East. Finally, towards the end of our first period when the accumulation of wealth in Great Britain was leading Englishmen to scan the world for placements for long-term investment of capital funds, the potentialities of China as a field for investment in railway and mining enterprise began to engage serious attention. The exploitation of this field for investment is inseparable from political complications, at all events when the country which receives the investment is not fully its own master. In this manner British relations with China tended to lose their purely commercial complexion and acquire more and more a political tinge.

Meanwhile the exposure of China's weakness in her war with Japan in 1894-95 encouraged those Powers which had territorial ambitions in Eastern Asia to press forward with their political plans. Russia, who ever since the Crimean War had been turning her attention to eastward expansion, had carried the construction of the trans-Siberian railway almost up to the Manchurian frontier and was already feeling her way southward in search of a warm-water port. Germany, who had started to build her navy, was similarly looking for a site for a naval base in Far Eastern waters, and France—who, like Russia, had had her expansionist ambitions diverted to the Far East by a military débâcle in Europe—was energetically engaged in consolidating her hold in Indo-China. With China the magnet of all these dynamic forces, the Far East became for a decade or so after the Sino-Japanese war a world center of *haute politique,* and Great Britain became involved, whether she wished it or not, in an international struggle for territorial possessions and special "spheres" in China.

The struggle had two facets; it was partly a local scramble for economic advantage, partly the playing out on the Far Eastern stage of rivalries between the great European Powers, who were at that time actively engaged in grouping themselves into power-blocs. This latter aspect of Far Eastern relations, as a typical manifestation of a conflict of forces proper to Europe, is well brought out by Mr. Philip Joseph in an analysis of the crucial period from 1894 to 1900. He says of those six years:[15]

"They introduced a new problem—an additional area of conflict—to international politics. Prior to 1894 political events in China were matters of comparative unimportance for the Chancelleries of Europe. China was regarded as a static unit, which did not affect the European political system called the balance of power. But the prospect of dividing up the Chinese state altered this point of view. After 1894, Chinese affairs were matters of deep concern to all those statesmen who were interested in the aggrandizement of their territories or in maintaining the status and prestige which their country had already attained. The addition of the Chinese Question to those already occupying the attention of diplomats made international politics more complicated and more acute than it already was. The Chinese Question ceased to be a question solely affecting China; it became an international one—in which the principal contenders were the Great Powers, and not China. Thereafter, China and Europe

[15] P. Joseph: *Foreign Diplomacy in China, 1894-1900,* Allen & Unwin, London, 1928, pp. 416-17.

were fused into one political system. Henceforth European politics could not be divorced from Chinese affairs. To understand one it was necessary to understand the other. The scope of the diplomats' activity was increased. They were compelled to follow carefully every change in the political barometer in China and Europe—for the political situation in one sphere affected the situation in the other. And, indeed, the necessity to realize a policy in Europe often compelled statesmen to make sacrifices in China. Nor has this been a temporary phase in the political system. It has been a relationship to world affairs which has continued until the present day."

The passage is given here at length because it implies an important truth which is fully as pertinent to the situation today as to that which existed when the words were written, namely that Far Eastern policy is essentially part of Great Britain's general world policy, and that it is always liable to find itself at the mercy of conditions arising in Europe or in other parts of the world.

To follow out in any detail the world aspects of British Far Eastern policy would, however, carry us too far afield. It must suffice to say that the Far East played a very important part in the opening movements of the regrouping of world forces which followed Great Britain's abandonment of her old policy of "splendid isolation," and which brought about the political alignment of the Great Powers of Europe which persisted up to the time of the Great War.

Here we must confine ourselves to tracing the effect which the incursion of European politics into the Far Eastern area had upon the general direction of British policy on the spot. The most striking change which it brought about—though it was of only temporary duration—was the relaxation of the policy of Chinese integrity. So long as there was a hope of the Chinese Government remaining sufficient master of its own house to act itself as guardian of the "open door" and to resist Russian advance (which was feared in England as part of Russia's southward drive through Asia towards the frontiers of India), so long it was a primary tenet of British policy to preserve the integrity of China. But once it had become, or had appeared to have become, impossible to save China from dismemberment, then British statesmen, if they wished to prevent the "freezing out" of British commercial interest in that country, had to contract their outlook and be ready to take a part in the staking out of claims. This became, in fact, for the time a feature of their policy, and the British Government were duly found taking part in the "battle of Concessions," the competition for spheres of interest and in the race for territorial acquisitions. That it was a role undertaken *malgré soi* was shown both by the British Government's attempts to set limits to the partitioning movement, especially in the Agreement concluded with Germany on October 16, 1900,[16] by which the contracting parties agreed to uphold the "open door" principle in China, disclaimed territorial designs upon China and arranged to consult together for action "in case of another Power making use of the complications in China (i.e., the Boxer Rebellion) in order to obtain any form whatever of territorial advantages." How firmly wedded the British Government were to the traditional principle of Chinese integrity, even at a time when they were being forced to yield to pressure to follow along the road of encroachment, is shown in a dispatch addressed by Lord Salisbury to the British Ambassador in St. Petersburg under the date of January 27, 1898.[17]

"The two Empires of China and Turkey," he wrote, "are so weak that in all important matters they are constantly guided by the advice of Foreign Powers. In giving this advice Russia and England are constantly opposed, neutralizing each other's efforts much more frequently than the real antagonism of their interests would justify; and this condition of things is not likely to diminish, but to increase. It is to remove or lessen this evil that we have thought an understanding with Russia might benefit both nations. We contemplate no infraction of existing rights. We would not . . . impair the integrity of the present empires of either China or Turkey. These two conditions are vital. We aim at no partition of territory, but only a partition of preponderance."

Soon afterwards the Under-Secretary of State told the House of Commons that "the integrity and independence of China . . . may be considered the cardinal bases of our policy."

The decline from this principle which, as we have seen, was now to come about is perhaps best explained by a quotation from Lord Salisbury's speech of May 4, 1898.[18] He referred to China as belonging to the category of "dying" Powers (the "sickman" of Turkey being, of course, the other moribund patient) and he added:

[16] British Treaty Series, 1901, No. 1. See also p. 26 below, footnote 26.
[17] Quoted in Joseph: *op. cit.*, p. 244.
[18] Quoted in Joseph: *op. cit.*, p. 317.

"Of course, it is not to be supposed that any one nation of the living nations will be allowed to have the profitable monopoly of curing or cutting up these unfortunate patients, and the controvery is as to who shall have the privilege of doing so, and in what measure he shall do it . . . Undoubtedly we shall not allow England to be at a disadvantage in any rearrangement that may take place."

To prevent others from seizing for themselves a monopoly of cutting up the patient (in the language of Lord Salisbury), Great Britain in the course of the next few months entered into agreements with other Powers for the recognition of spheres of interest in China and extorted from the Peking Government, under barely veiled threats of force, the grant of railway concessions, and cessions of territory, as "compensation" for what had been given to other Powers. But this action must be regarded as at most a temporary aberration, induced by forces beyond her control, from the traditional lines of Great Britain's Far Eastern policy, which reasserted themselves[19] as soon as circumstances allowed—as soon, that is, as the danger of pre-emption by other Powers ceased to be imminent. Of this transient phase of Great Britain's Far Eastern policy Mr. Joseph[20] pertinently remarks that it

"was no longer a free and independent policy. It was forced upon her by the action of the four other Powers, in particular by the refusal of Germany and Japan to block the advance of Russia in China. Henceforth Britain was prepared, if need be, to make territorial acquisitions in China, to safeguard her commercial interests there and in general to maintain the balance of power. This action naturally ran counter to her policy of maintaining the territorial integrity of China . . . but it was a policy initiated by the other Powers and one which the British Government had foreseen it might have to adopt."

An authoritative writer, Mr. William L. Langer, of Harvard University, sums up the position more briefly by saying: "It must be concluded then that the British, while desiring the

[19] Reasserted themselves, that is to say, in regard to China *inside the Wall*. The "open door" and "Chinese integrity" doctrine were never effectively restored as against Russian and Japanese encroachments in the extra-mural regions. Indeed British recognition of Russian predominance in Mongolia and North Manchuria became a bargaining counter to induce Russia to be amenable to British views in regard to Persia and Tibet, and when, after the Russo-Japanese War, these two Powers came together and arranged between themselves for the mutual recognition of "spheres" in Manchuria and Mongolia, the British Government tacitly acquiesced.

[20] Joseph: *op. cit.,* p. 293.

integrity of China, were prepared to see this principle infringed to a certain extent by other powers to prevent its being discarded entirely."[21]

There was no pretense that Great Britain's interest in Chinese integrity was purely altruistic. It was openly and admittedly based primarily on concern for her own interests. Mr. Joseph Chamberlain stated this clearly in a speech which he made at Manchester at the end of the crucial year 1898.[22] "We did not think," he said "it was our business to appear as the champions of China, to defend her against the attacks which might be made upon her. The principle for which we did contend was that no acquisition of territory by any foreign Power should alter the existing state of things in this respect, that the markets of China should be open to fair and even competition to all through the open door."

It is necessary to say something at this point about the terms "sphere of interest" and "sphere of influence," which figured so largely in the diplomatic exchanges of this period of Far Eastern history. "Interest" and "influence" are, of course, not synonymous, though the greater, namely the second, may be regarded as comprising the less. Great Britain had long possessed an important sphere of interest in the Yangtze Valley where her share of trade, industry, and finance far exceeded that of all her rivals put together. The Yangtze Valley, however, was not, and never became, a sphere of influence, in its strict sense, for Great Britain or for any other Power. A "sphere of influence" in China is defined by Mr. G. F. Hudson in *The Far East in World Politics*[23] as "a region of the Chinese Empire within which a particular foreign power was granted a preferential or exclusive right to capital investment enterprises, especially concessions for railway construction." The staking out of such spheres of influence by France in the South West, Germany in Shantung and Russia in the North, and the attempts made by these Powers to dominate vast areas of China by means of railways constructed, owned and operated by foreign Governments constituted a direct challenge to the traditional British principles of

[21] In *The Diplomacy of Imperialism, 1890-1902*, Knopf, New York, 1935, 2 vols., p. 461.
[22] Quoted in Joseph: *op. cit.*, p. 379.
[23] G. F. Hudson: *The Far East in World Politics*, Oxford University Press, 1937.

the Open Door and integrity of China and a serious threat to the British sphere of interest in the Yangtze Valley. In the absence of American support at this stage in maintaining the Open Door in China, the British Government decided that they could not, alone and unsupported, prevent the establishment of spheres of influence in general. They reacted vigorously, however, against attempts to encroach on the British sphere of interest in the Yangtze Valley, and fought to prevent the heart of China becoming a sphere of influence for the benefit of any foreign Power. The French and the Russians planned to extend their Government-owned railways from south and north respectively into the heart of China, meeting at Hankow on the Yangtze. Great Britain insisted on the abandonment of this scheme. She demanded for herself a number of important railways in this region, but on a non-proprietary basis, the lines being built by British concessionnaires with loaned captal as commercial enterprises for, and on behalf of, the Chinese Government as the owner, the loan interest being charged in the first instance on the traffic receipts. When Germany, France, and Russia then proceeded to seize ports and stake out spheres of influence in the regions in which the ports were situated, the British Government set their face against any such seizure of ports on the Yangtze river. They accordingly obtained from the Chinese Government a declaration that no territory in the Yangtze Valley would be alienated to any other Power, thus securing "the retention in Chinese possession of the Yangtze region, now entirely hers, as providing security for the free course and development of trade."[24]

During this period Great Britain obtained from China the lease of Weihaiwei "for as long as Russia remained in occupation of Port Arthur," and also a lease for 99 years of the territory of Kowloon adjoining the colony of Hongkong. This action is undoubtedly open to criticism as a contribution to the "partitionist" tendency. Its description as a derogation from the principle of the Open Door is, however, unwarranted. In neither case was there any grant of prior rights in the adjacent region. Kowloon was taken solely to improve the defensive

[24] Exchange of Notes between Sir Claud MacDonald and the Tsungli Yamen dated February 9, 1898.

position of Hongkong and Weihaiwei was made a British naval station in the belief that it would act as a counterpoise to Russia and so help to maintain both the Open Door and the integrity of China. The American Government, it is instructive to note, viewed the situation in exactly the same light. At the beginning of 1898 the United States Government were not prepared to cooperate with England in maintaining the Open Door,[25] but after the war with Spain America began to play a more active part in the Far East. Mr. Conger, the American Minister in Peking, urged upon his Government the view that the door could not be kept open if America merely stood aside. His view was that America should own and control at least one good port in China as "a strong foothold" in order to "keep permanently open doors for our commerce." On September 6, 1899, John Hay, the United States Secretary of State, wrote the famous Open Door notes to which further reference will be made on a later page. On July 3, 1900, when the Legations in Peking were being besieged during the Boxer rising, he sent a circular note to the Powers asking them to collaborate in seeking a solution which would preserve Chinese territorial and administrative entity and safeguard the principle of the Open Door and equal opportunity. Four months later he instructed Mr. Conger to obtain from the Chinese Government the grant of a naval base and territorial concession in the province of Fukien. The proposal fell through because China had given a promise to Japan never to alienate any part of Fukien. It may be fairly supposed, however, that Mr. Hay acted in the belief that such a foothold would prevent the disintegration of China and serve as a guarantee of the Open Door.

The turn of the century saw the development of another of those essential features of British policy of which we spoke before, namely that of the "balance of power." The British statesmen of the day, notably Mr. Joseph Chamberlain, had, in the last decade of the nineteenth century, become convinced that Great Britain must abandon her traditional position of aloofness and look for a partner or partners for mutual help against a possible aggressor. Russia, in particular, was regarded as a danger in view of the designs on India which she was believed to entertain. The first *pourparlers* engaged in were

[25] See Langer, *op. cit.*, p. 472.

with Germany. These broke down,[26] but not before a German suggestion to include Japan in the proposed alliance had opened the way for Anglo-Japanese negotiations, which duly fructified in the first Anglo-Japanese treaty of January 20, 1902. From the British point of view the Alliance was primarily intended as a counter-weight against Russia, a purpose which it fulfilled to perfection by "holding the ring" for the single-handed defeat of Russia by Japan in the Far East. After the Russian defeat, the Alliance (into which the treaty was expanded at its renewals in 1905 and 1911) continued to serve the same general purpose by providing a lever, this time against Germany, when the German navy began to grow into a serious rival.[27]

The high political tension in the Far East calmed down early in the new century as the result of the check given to Russia by her defeat by Japan and by the general understandings which were arrived at between Great Britain, France, and Russia and which grew in the fullness of time into the Triple Entente. The center of gravity of international politics shifted away from the Far East, commercial interests became once more supreme, and commercial influences recovered their force in the direction of British Far Eastern policy. Owing to the fact that this was the great period of railway financing in China, it was the banking and allied interests which in this respect played the most active part. These interests tended strongly towards internationalism

---

[26] The Anglo-German "anti-partition" Agreement of October 16, 1900, which has been referred to above and which—together with the Convention of November 14, 1898, by which Great Britain waived her claims to Samoa in favor of Germany—was the only concrete product of the attempted Anglo-German *rapprochement* in so far as the Far East was concerned, proved abortive when Great Britain wished to invoke it against Russian penetration in Manchuria. Germany, in fact, refused to be drawn directly into the silent struggle between England and Russia.

[27] It would be wrong, of course, to represent the Anglo-Japanese Alliance as engendered, on the British side, solely by the need to adjust the scales in the matter of military power. A predisposition towards partnership had already been created by other circumstances and events, particularly by such gestures of British goodwill towards Japan as the initiative taken by the British Government in renouncing extraterritorial rights in Japan and the British refusal to join in the action of the *Dreibund* when the latter obliged Japan to reduce her territorial demands on China after the war of 1894-5, also by the common interest which both countries had in preserving the Chinese "open door" during the period of Franco-Russian encroachment. For a general survey of the diplomacy of this period see *China and Japan*, Information Department Papers, Royal Institute of International Affairs, London, No. 21A, Third edition, 1941.

and in some instances—e.g., collaboration between the British and German banks in China—they tended in a direction which was patently at variance with the general lines of Great Britain's policy in the world at large. They were at the same time, through the building up of international organs such as the "China Consortium," paving the way towards the collective treatment of Chinese affairs which reached its consummation in the postwar Washington agreements.

There had long been a rapprochement between British and American views in regard to China, and relations were drawn still closer by the extremely benevolent neutrality adopted by Great Britain in the Spanish-American war and her sympathetic attitude to the United States claim to the Philippines. In November 1898 Lord Salisbury took occasion to speak in public of the advantage to Great Britain of America's entry into the colonial field. At the same time there was talk in the American press of the possibility of an Anglo-American alliance,[28] and Mr. Joseph Chamberlain went so far as to say, in his speech at Manchester on November 16, 1898, which has been quoted before, that Great Britain, needing "collective influence" behind her "Open Door" policy, might well look to the United States for closer cooperation, and he expressed his belief that "a combination between the two great English-speaking peoples . . . would be a guarantee for the peace and civilization of the world."

On the American side, the annexation of the Philippines— their first colonial possession—had provided the occasion for a formulation of the Government's policy in respect to the principle of the "Open Door." In instructions to the American Peace Commissioners President McKinley wrote "we seek no advantages in the Orient which are not common to all. Asking only the 'open door' to others," thus virtually paraphrasing declarations made by the British Government on many earlier occasions.

The general identity of American and British aims and ideals found expression in the Open Door notes which Mr. John Hay addressed a year later to the Governments concerned in China's affairs. In his Note to the British Foreign Office the American Secretary of State began by recognizing that it was "the settled

[28] The *New York Times,* November 11, 1898, quoted in Joseph: *op. cit.,* p. 377.

policy and purpose of Great Britain not to use any privileges
which may be granted to it in China as a means of excluding
commercial rivals, and that freedom of trade for it in that
Empire means freedom of trade for all the world alike" and
that "the British Government had sought to maintain what is
commonly called the 'open door' policy"; he then proceeded to
invite British participation in a declaration designed to give
specific shape to the "Open Door" principle, "believing that the
action is in entire harmony with its (the British Government's)
consistent theory and purpose." To this invitation the British
Government acceded with an offer to make the desired declaration when the remaining Powers should have agreed. This they
did, and on March 20, 1899, the American Secretary of State
was able to announce that he had received satisfactory replies
from all the Powers to whom his notes had been addressed.

In the Hay Notes the United States Government adopted
substantially the same attitude as that attributed to the British
Government by Professor Langer in the quotation from his
book given a few pages back, namely that while desiring the
integrity of China, they were prepared to see the principle
infringed to a certain extent by other Powers to prevent its
being discarded entirely. The Notes recognized that existing
spheres of influence were accomplished facts and even that
further such spheres might be carved out in future. All that
the Powers were asked to promise was that in existing or future
spheres of influence they would not "interfere with any treaty
port or vested interest," that the Chinese treaty tariff would
continue to apply and the duties continue to be levied by the
Chinese Government and that there would be no discrimination
as regards harbor dues and railway rates.

It is hardly necessary to refute the suggestion sometimes made
by less well-informed writers that the "Hay Notes" were the
origin of the Open Door doctrine in relation to China, but
attention may usefully be drawn to a recent article in the *Far
Eastern Quarterly*[29] showing that, long before the Nanking
Treaty, the Open Door principle inspired Great Britain's deal-
ings with China partly at least as a means of consolidating foreign interests to meet the obstructive attitude of the Chinese
authorities of those days. Passing on to the 1894-98 period, when

[29] *Far Eastern Quarterly* of February 1942: "Origin of most-favoured nation
and open door policies in China" by Earl H. Pritchard of Wayne University.

the doctrine fell into abeyance and the "scramble" for concessions took place, the writer says "the new development ran
counter to the interests of both England and the United States
and they wished to resist it. America's refusal to enter into
downright cooperation with England prevented really effective
measures from being taken to maintain the old Open Door"; he
concludes that "the Open Door doctrine promulgated by the
United States in 1899 was a poor compromise which aimed only
to protect established commercial interests and neglected
entirely the Open Door in regard to financial and other
matters."

The *détente* after the Russo-Japanese War left Great Britain
free to decide her attitude towards an important development
which was becoming evident in the Far East, the growth of the
revolutionary movement in China. When this came to a head
in 1911 the British reaction was two-fold. British feeling was
constitutionally sympathetic to democratic movements for
liberty and reform, and the British Government were on this
principle definitely adverse to foreign support for buttressing
up the Manchu dynasty in China, or for restoring it after it
had fallen. But Great Britain's immediate interest lay in the
greatest possible preservation of Chinese internal order and
administrative continuity as a guarantee for the safety of her
large vested interests. The consequence was that British policy—
not uninfluenced by the views of the British finance houses
which were actively concerned with Chinese loans—threw its
weight on the side of the conservative elements in North China,
and encouraged international loans for the support of the
Peking régime. By so doing it alienated the radical party in
Canton, thus laying the foundations of the anti-British outburst
which occurred in the following decade. In the light of subsequent history it might not unjustly be said that Great Britain
made the same political miscalculation which she made in
regard to the Young Turk movement and "backed the wrong
horse."[30] The policy adopted owed something, undoubtedly, to
the fortuitous fact that the foreign Representatives in China,
resident in Peking at a week's journey from Canton, were in far
closer contact with the northern reactionaries than with the
revolutionaries of the south. Towards China as a whole the

[30] There is, of course, always the question whether the "horse" if backed by
Great Britain (instead of by Russia) would have won!

policy of the British Foreign Office had been developing along increasingly liberal lines. This was exemplified by the terms of the "Mackay" Treaty of 1903. By envisaging for the first time the relinquishment of extra-territorial rights and privileges as soon as orderly conditions prevailed, the 1903 Treaty foreshadowed, however faintly, the policy of putting an end to foreign tutelage and of hastening forward Chinese administrative autonomy—a policy which was accepted in principle at the Washington Conference of 1921 and took practical form in the "Chamberlain memorandum" of December 1926.[31]

3. Third Phase: The Period of the Great War of 1914-18

The next phase, that of the Great War, can be dealt with very briefly for the simple reason that no valid conclusions can be drawn from the records of a period when British Far Eastern policy was completely subordinated to the all-absorbing aim of winning the war. The British commercial interest in the Far East was largely eclipsed owing to the dislocation of industry and transport; security in the "long-term" sense had ceased to be of account for a nation which was actually in the midst of a life-and-death struggle, while the preservation of peace, as a goal of policy, had no meaning when there was no peace to preserve. British diplomacy in the Far East was therefore temporarily bereft of its standing objectives and became, for the time being, ancillary to British war strategy, and as such need not detain us except for an allusion to the Government's reaction to Japan's Twenty-One Demands. The demands, as presented to Yuan Shih-kai on January 18, 1915, consisted of five groups, of which the first four related to Shantung, Manchuria, and Inner Mongolia, mining and railway concessions in Central China and the non-alienation of coastal harbors, et cetera, while the fifth group contained extremely far-reaching demands involving Japanese political, economic, and military tutelage of China. Both the British and American Governments, as soon as they got wind of the demands, exerted on the Japanese Government informal pressure which, added to the resistance which the Peking régime was offering to the Japanese, caused the latter to drop Group V. on the face-saving pretence that this group, as distinct from the other four, represented only Japanese "wishes." When they, however, on May 7 presented

[31] See below, p. 35.

China with an ultimatum to enforce the "revised" demands, and so brought dangerously near the prospect of a Sino-Japanese war, Lord Grey immediately handed a memorandum to the Japanese Ambassador expressing his Government's deep concern at this prospect which, as he stated, imperiled the independence and integrity of China, one of the main objects of the Anglo-Japanese Alliance. By virtue of Article I of the treaty of alliance the Japanese Government were invited to consult with the British Government and to give them the opportunity of promoting a friendly settlement.[32]

Thus the British Government used the alliance as a lever for restraining Japan, at the same time that the United States Government, being differently placed, adopted for the same purpose the method of "non-recognition." The State Department did this a week after the date of Lord Grey's memorandum by sending identic notes to the Japanese and Chinese Governments refusing to recognize agreements impairing the treaty rights of the United States, the integrity of China, or the Open Door policy.

The danger of war with which the British memorandum concerned itself primarily was actually averted by China's acceptance of the Japanese ultimatum, which occurred in the interval between Lord Grey's action and that of the State Department. Japan's more drastic designs on China having been successfully frustrated, Great Britain, her hands full with her war with Germany, refrained from taking further repressive steps. For this, indeed, she had but little encouragement in the attitude of her friends and associates at that time. Czarist Russia was pursuing a policy of conciliation of Japan which was presently to lead to their *entente* of July 3 of the following year, while America, already moving along the path which ended in her entry into the European struggle, was, as Professor Toynbee remarks in his *Survey of International Affairs*,[33] "more unwilling than ever to risk incurring commitments in other quarters." He goes on to observe that "when she eventually became a belligerent she became almost as anxious as her European Associates to cultivate Japan's good will," as evidenced by the Lansing-Ishii exchange of notes in November

[32] Quoted in the *Far Eastern Policy of the United States* by A. Whitney Griswold, p. 196.

[33] *Survey of International Affairs for 1920-1923*, p. 424.

1917, which gave qualified recognition to Japan's special interest in China based on territorial propinquity, and later by America's endorsement at the Versailles Conference of the wartime pledges given by the Allies to Japan regarding the succession to Germany's rights and titles in Shantung.

Having dealt thus briefly with British diplomacy in the Far East during the war period, we may now proceed to consider the new problems with which British policy was faced in the Far East after the restoration of peace, and the manner in which they were met.

4. *Fourth Phase: From 1919 till the Manchurian Affair of 1931*

Of British policy in the Far East from 1919 onwards one general observation may be made—that its dominating aim was stability. The time for thinking in terms of British "expansionism" or "imperialism"—the "door-forcing" period in fact—had finally passed. Henceforth the British interest was to prevent sudden and violent changes and to ensure that such modifications of the *status quo* as had to occur should be brought about peaceably and with the least possible upset. For this nothing was more necessary than a united, peaceful, and prosperous China able to hold her own in the world.

In the Far East the situation to which this doctrine had to be applied was, meanwhile, radically altered. With the eclipse of Russia and Germany as effective "Far Eastern Powers" the balance of forces was now a completely new one. Japan had emerged from the war as the potentially dominant Power in Eastern Asia, while China, for her part, was touching the "low point" of helplessness and political disruption. The United States was greatly increasing her relative naval importance in the Pacific; she was on bad terms with Japan, and "Japan's conflict with America took the center of the stage."[34]

The situation in regard to British security in the Pacific had simultaneously taken on a new complexion owing to the expansion of Japanese naval power. Whereas in the past Great Britain, when considering the dangers of hostile action in that area, had

[34] G. F. Hudson: *The Far East in World Politics*, Oxford University Press, 1937, p. 185. An additional factor in the situation which called for consideration was that, in reference to Japan, the views of the Canadian Government—to which, as to those of all the Dominions, the British Government had as the result of the War become incomparably more susceptible—were more or less closely aligned with those of the United States.

had to reckon only with the navies of European Powers operating under the same handicaps of geographical remoteness as
her own navy, she now had to take far greater account of a
Power whose home bases lay in the Pacific itself and whose
striking radius embraced the British possessions in that ocean,
as the future was to show only too clearly. That Power had
during the war pursued an aggressive policy in Asia very
harmful to British interests, both existing and prospective, and
her Russian neighbor was no longer in a state to check her in
further encroachments.

Meanwhile the China market offered one of the most hope-
ful adjuncts to the postwar recovery of British industry restored to a peace footing, and the Far East had lost none of
its commercial importance for Great Britain and could from that
standpoint by no means be simply ignored.

The problems before Great Britain were thus urgent and
manifold. For the safeguarding of British interests as a whole
two lines of policy presented themselves. One possible course
was to rely upon continued partnership with Japan as an assurance against any threat to British possessions and lines of communications, and, despite the unpromising experience of the
Twenty-One Demands, to proceed on the hope of Great Britain
being able to use the moderating influence of an ally to curb
further attempts by Japan to exploit the weakness of China for
monopolistic purposes;[35] the other course was to try to achieve
stability in the Far East by means of a multilateral understanding embracing all the Powers concerned. Influenced by many
considerations and not least by the disastrous possibility of
finding herself the ally of a country which might have drifted
into war with the United States—where, as also in Canada, a
strong anti-Japanese sentiment prevailed and where racial feeling and the immigration question were particularly embittering
relations—the British Government preferred the second of the
two alternatives. They cooperated with the United States to
bring about a multilateral agreement and at the same time
terminated the alliance with Japan.

The Washington Agreements which resulted were for Great
Britain an "omnibus" guarantee (for whatever it might be

[35] In 1938 a minority section of British opinion was advancing the view
that the disastrous situation which had arisen in the Far East could have been
averted if Great Britain had adhered to the Anglo-Japanese Alliance.

worth) of most of the things which touched her interests most deeply—the "Open Door," equal opportunity, Chinese integrity, and—through the Naval Limitation Treaty and the Four-Power Agreement—security. The military provisions of the treaties were calculated to assure to each of the three Powers a position of naval predominance in its own sphere. The maintenance of peace in the Far East, as in the world generally, had already, it was hoped, been assured by the collective action provisions of the League of Nations Covenant. To provide physical security—the security, that is to say, of British possessions and sea-communications in the Pacific—the Treaties were not, however, sufficient in themselves, and the British Government deemed it necessary to supplement the safeguards which they afforded by proceeding with the construction of a first-class naval and air base at Singapore,[36] in order to guard the gate into the Indian Ocean and to supply the requisite jumping-off place for any military action which it might become necessary to take in the Pacific. Broadly speaking, from the British point of view the effect of the Washington Treaties was to internationalize the business of safeguarding British interests in the Far East inasmuch as their protection would depend from now onwards on the faithful observance of a series of multilateral self-denying ordinances, chief among which was the Nine-Power Agreement.

Looking back from the standpoint of later years one can make an approximate appraisal of the efficacy of this policy of internationalization. Taking first the question of security, the establishment of naval ratios at Washington, which was later extended by the London Naval Agreement of 1930, gave the British Admiralty a period of peace of mind,[37] but (as must always be the case with armament limitation agreements) its value ended as soon as it ceased to correspond to the views of one of the signatory parties concerning its national "defense" needs. Japan's denunciation of the Treaty at the end of 1936

---

[36] The plan to create such a base was included in the recommendations of Lord Jellicoe after his visit to the Far East in 1919. A decision on the subject was deferred during the Washington Conference but was taken after its close in 1922. The Labour Government which came into power in 1924 suspended the work, but it was resumed by the succeeding Conservative Government in the spring of the following year.

[37] In so far as it contributed to the neglect of British armaments in the years before 1936, this may be regarded as a "doubtful blessing."

left Great Britain embarrassed in the Pacific by an unregulated situation full of uncertainty at a time when she was already facing the consequences of the breakdown of the collective security system.

As a guarantee for what Great Britain desired to see accomplished in China, the Nine-Power Agreement failed[38] in bringing about what Great Britain most needed, namely a China at peace with herself and well-disposed to Great Britain. Consequently when Great Britain found herself faced in 1925-6 with a violent anti-British agitation, it became imperative for the British Government to strike out an individual line of policy. This was boldly undertaken by Sir Austin Chamberlain, who was then Foreign Secretary. In his memorandum of December 18, 1926,[39] communicated to the Governments of the Washington Powers, Sir Austen enunciated a policy of recognizing the justice of the Chinese claim for treaty revision and abandoning the old attitude of rigid insistence on the strict letter of treaty rights. Without "waiting for or insisting on the prior establishment of a strong Central Government" (to use Sir Austen's own words) the British Government undertook to proceed with the gradual liquidation of the "unequal treaties," thus assisting China along the road to full recovery of sovereignty. At the Washington Conference the Powers had paid lip service to the principle of respect for China's sovereignty but had continued to act as if it was the normal and natural state of things that China should be kept in leading strings. The Memorandum accordingly exhorted the Powers not to force foreign control upon an unwilling China and to abandon the idea that the economic and political rehabilitation of China could only be secured under foreign tutelage.

Explaining the policy in a speech to his constituents, Sir Austen, after referring to the fact that the old treaty system (of which, as he said, "we were the principal architects") was manifestly growing antiquated, and after describing the steps which the British Government were prepared to take to revise it, observed:

[38] It was a failure which can be attributed equally to the continuance of the Chinese civil war and to the dilatoriness of the signatory Powers in implementing the provisions for freeing China from foreign "servitudes."

[39] *The Times,* December 28, 1926. For the relevant extract see Appendix II.

"we are going more than half-way, but I am certain that this is a right
and wise course. We do not disguise from ourselves the inconveniences
and the difficulties of the moment, but we are thinking of our relations
with China for the next 100 years."

This new policy has been justifiably described by a recent
writer[40] as a "triumph of enlightened common sense." Its
implementation was begun without delay by the British Government, who took the lead in recognizing the new Kuomintang Government of China, in conceding tariff autonomy, and
in negotiating for the early abolition of extra-territorial rights,
and at the same time handed back to Chinese administration the
British Concessions at Hankow and Kiukiang.

The effect of the "Washington" policy on British relations
with Japan could hardly be other than unfavorable. There was
a natural resentment in Japan at the defection of her old ally
and much dissatisfaction was created in influential Japanese
circles by the naval agreements with their denial of Japanese
equality, and by the resumption of work on the Singapore base.
Meanwhile closer relations with the United States, which might
have provided a measure of compensation for the drift away
from Japan, was obstructed by the growth of American isolationist sentiment.

On an all-round judgement, however, the Nine-Power Treaty,
by acting as the guardian of the principle of the "Open Door"
and equal opportunity in China,[41] was reasonably efficacious in
serving British requirements up to the close of the "pre-Man-
churian" period, and it laid the necessary ground for the liberal
forward policy initiated in 1926 which was to prove a sound
piece of statesmanship.

[40] Sir Eric Teichman: *Affairs of China*, London, Methuen, 1938, p. 49.

[41] The distinction must again be emphasized between intra- and extra-mural
China. Japan's claim to a "special position" in Manchuria and Inner Mongolia
received qualified recognition in the China Consortium agreement of 1920.

CHAPTER III

SINCE THE MANCHURIAN AFFAIR

1. *Up to the Outbreak of War in Europe*

The reason for taking the Manchurian Affair as the starting point of a new era for the purpose of this study was implied in what has been written on the last page of the Introduction, but a little amplification is needed. From 1931 onwards British policy represented to an ever-increasing extent the British reaction to Japan's challenge in East Asia. It is true that the challenge existed already before the Manchurian Affair, having declared itself in, *inter alia,* the Twenty-One Demands, and also that there were periods after the Manchurian Affair when the Japanese challenge sank temporarily into the background. It is true, too, that certain important developments in British policy in the "post-Manchuria" era were undertaken without special reference to the menace from Japan. Yet, taken by and large, British Far Eastern policy from 1931 onwards can be interpreted in terms of Japan's challenge in East Asia and Great Britain's response to that challenge.

Leaving aside the inevitable accompaniments of dislocation of trade and accidental injury to third-party life and property, Japan's challenge may be discribed under the following seven heads:

(1) The curtailing of China's territorial and administrative sovereignty, the preservation of which had repeatedly been declared to be the object of British policy in China; (2) the closing of the "Open Door" in Manchuria by the creation of trading and manufacturing monopolies, the introduction of exchange restrictions, and other administrative acts, and the extension of similar economic barriers to foreign enterprise in parts of China dominated by Japan; (3) the occupation and control of Chinese railways and other means of communication, and the taking over of Chinese national sources of revenue (including a major portion of the Maritime Customs collections, which provided the security for the service of Chinese

foreign loans); (4) interference with the rights, privileges, and operations of foreign individuals and foreign administrative bodies in China's treaty ports; (5) in the wider sphere of world politics—the blow which in and after 1931 Japan dealt to the League principle of the peaceful settlement of disputes and to the whole system of collective security by her resort to force and her disregard of those international obligations upon which the collective system was built; (6) the denunciation of the naval treaty, occupation of new strategic bases, and so forth, upsetting the equilibrium of power at which Great Britain had aimed by means of the "Washington Treaties"; (7) Japan's association with Germany by adhering to the Anti-Comintern Pact and so adding herself more positively than before to the number of Great Britain's potential enemies threatening British security. Finally Japan's challenge summed itself up in her claim and attempt to establish a so-called "New Order in East Asia."

There were three theoretically conceivable methods of meeting Japan's challenge. One would have been to try to purchase immunity from the effects of Japanese aggression by standing aloof and not attempting to frustrate her; another would have been to plunge into active opposition, applying coercive measures backed by the necessary preparedness to face a consequent war; the third was to exercise a general restraint on Japan wherever and whenever possible without inviting an armed clash and to deal severally with the problems raised by her aggressive actions as they occurred.

The first was directly contrary to the general policy of Great Britain; it would never have been countenanced by British opinion and it certainly never came under contemplation by the Government. The second involved risks which the British Government, in the conditions which then prevailed, could not contemplate. This was frankly explained by the Foreign Secretary on December 21, 1937 when replying to a plea by the Leader of the Opposition in the House of Commons for the exercise of more drastic pressure on Japan.[1]

"If," Mr. Eden said, "hon. Members opposite are advocating sanctions by the League . . . I would remind them that there are two possible forms of sanctions—the ineffective, which are not worth putting on, and the effective, which means the risk, if not the certainty, of war. I say deliberately that nobody could contemplate any action of that kind in

[1] *Hansard,* December 21, 1937, cols. 1883-4.

the Far East unless they are convinced that they have overwhelming force to back their policy. Do right hon. gentlemen opposite really think that the League of Nations today, with only two great naval Powers in it, ourselves and France, have got that overwhelming force? It must be quite clear to every one that that overwhelming force does not exist . . . Every nation at Geneva from the beginning of this dispute knows perfectly well that the very thought of action of any kind in the Far East must depend on the co-operation of other nations besides those who are actually Members of the League at this time . . . The League depends upon the acceptance by the general body of the great nations of the world, of the rule of law in some form, and that when you have, as you have to-day, Japan who clearly by her action does not accept that rule of law, and Germany who, at any rate, will not join in the League to co-operate in enforcing that rule of law, and . . . the United States, who though sympathetic to the rule of law, are not prepared to undertake commitments, all these factors must clearly have their effect upon the authority of the League."

Since neither of the two more positive courses of action was within the scope of practical politics, the Government were restricted to the third, involving the continuance of their support of the National Government in China while at the same time endeavoring to promote agreement between China and Japan. This may be regarded as a middle way, and a reasonable one, between intervention and inaction. Since this policy naturally involved elasticity in its adjustment to conditions on the spot, it can best be examined, not chronologically, but in its relation to a few of the various types of test to which it was submitted.

We may conveniently start with the issue which arose first in point of time, the undermining by Japan's action in China of the principles established by the League of Nations Covenant and by the various Peace Treaties. This cannot, of course, be entirely separated from other cognate issues, such as the threat to local British interests through Japanese encroachments on Chinese territory and Chinese governmental authority, but it stands by itself to this extent that the issue was one which had to be handled internationally at Geneva, and that British policy expressed itself in the form of cooperation with other Members of the League.

In dealing with this international aspect of the Manchurian conflict the British Government based their policy on loyalty to the principles of the League Covenant. The most unequivocal of the many declarations which they made to this effect was

the statement in a speech made by the British Foreign Secretary
before the Assembly of the League on December 7, 1932, when
he said:

"so far as the desire and the determination to act as loyal Members of
the League of Nations are concerned, for all of us alike the Covenant of
the League of Nations is our constitutional law . . . we are not at liberty
to disregard it. We are bound to sustain it."

The charge has been leveled against the British Government,
in regard to their attitude towards the Sino-Japanese dispute
as a whole, that in practice they refused the risks inherent in
taking effective steps to preserve the collective system.[2] As
regards these inherent risks the critics have generally assumed
that if it became necessary for the League Powers to apply
military sanctions to Japan, the burden and risk would have
been shared among the Powers with military forces at their
disposal, in other words that American troops would have been
made available for despatch to the Far East and the American
Navy would have acted as the ally of the British Navy in any
measures which might have had to be taken. The weakness of
this assumption becomes clear when the state of American
opinion is examined as it has been by Mr. Stimson in his book
The Far Eastern Crisis.[3]

In such circumstances the British Government would obviously have been quite unwarranted in relying on the United
States taking positive action in support of collective security or
going beyond moral disapproval and the attempt to mobilize
world opinion. One sees on looking back that this was almost
the inevitable consequence of the policy which had been
adopted at the Washington Conference. Its effect had been, to
quote Professor Toynbee's words,[4] "to leave Japan physically
supreme in the Far East, on land and sea and in the air" and to
create a strategic position in which Japan was virtually immune
from any serious attack on the part of any Power holding
important potential hostages in the form of foreign holdings in
the Far East, and could, in the event of hostilities, strike at

[2] This criticism of British policy was fully elaborated in Professor Toynbee's
Survey of International Affairs, 1932, on pp. 517-8, 523-33, 538-58.

[3] H. L. Stimson: *The Far Eastern Crisis: Recollections and Observations,*
New York, Council on Foreign Relations, 1936. See particularly pp. 56, 76-7,
80, 84 and 94-5.

[4] *Survey of International Affairs, 1932,* p. 525.

Russia in the Maritime Province, at the United States in the Philippines, at France in Indo-China, and at the British Empire in Hongkong, Borneo and Malaya.

The strategic position as thus described, and the attitude of the United States and the U.S.S.R.—the two great Pacific Powers who were not Members of the League—caused it to be generally recognized when the Manchurian problem came on the table at Geneva that it was impracticable to apply sanctions as a means of restraining Japan, and in point of fact the League was not called upon to decide for or against sanctions since China never addressed the necessary appeal under Article 16 of the Covenant, nor was Japan ever named the aggressor.

In these circumstances the British Government followed the line of action initiated by the United States and used their influence in persuading the other Members of the League to accept the American doctrine of non-recognition of the fruits of aggression, which had been announced in the American Note of January 7, 1932, addressed to China and Japan. Consequently on January 29 the Council of the League, with the exception of the Chinese and Japanese representatives, drew up a declaration referring to the American Note of January 7 and stating that it would be impossible for the League to endorse a settlement secured by force. Then on February 16 the Council members, with the same exceptions, addressed a Note to Japan declaring that no infringement of territorial integrity, and no change in the political independence of any Member of the League brought about by force, would be recognized as valid and effectual by Members of the League. On March 7 the British Foreign Secretary, in a speech before the Assembly, proposed that the Assembly in order to come into line with the American attitude, should make a declaration reaffirming the principles of the Covenant and of the Kellogg Pact, and making it clear that changes brought about by means contrary to those principles "manifestly could not receive the approval of the Assembly." A resolution to this effect was duly passed on March 11. Its proposer was the British Foreign Secretary, and it formally adopted the non-recognition principle set out in the American Note of January 7.

The action taken by the British representatives on this occasion, as well as the fact that it was the British representative, Lord Lytton, who was elected Chairman of the Commission of

Enquiry sent by the League to Manchuria, are sufficient refutation of the suggestion which has often been made that Great Britain's role in handling the Manchurian Affair was essentially passive.

The charge has frequently been made that the British Government failed to "go along" with the United States Government in the action which the latter desired to take in the Manchurian conflict. It has raised much criticism and controversy, and at a later date the matter was thrashed out in the correspondence columns of the *Times*. In a letter published on November 10, 1938, Sir John Pratt, who at the time of the incident was Adviser to the Foreign Office on Far Eastern Affairs, explained that in February 1932, when Mr. Stimson put forward a proposal for a joint invocation of the Nine-Power Treaty, a written answer was returned stating that the British Government was most anxious to cooperate with America in this matter and explaining the steps that had immediately been taken to bring into line the other League Powers who were also signatories to the Nine-Power Treaty. Sir John Pratt attributed Mr. Stimson's impression that the British Government were reluctant to join in such a demarche to a lapse of memory on his part.

A letter followed from Mr. E. M. Gull, suggesting that Mr. Stimson's impression might have been caused by the British Government's action in rejecting his earlier proposal that they should address a note to the Japanese Government on the lines of the United States Note of January 7, 1932. He referred in particular to the Foreign Office *communiqué* published in the press on January 11, 1932, which, as Mr. Stimson had pointed out in *The Far Eastern Crisis,* was generally interpreted as a rebuff to the United States, and, comparing the *communiqué* with Mr. Stimson's Note to the Chinese and Japanese Governments, drew the conclusion that, in the first stage of the incident, the British Government did not "go along" with the Government of the United States. In a reply published in the *Times* on November 30, 1938, Sir John Pratt stated that on this occasion also a written reply had been sent to Mr. Stimson on January 9 explaining that Great Britain's position as a Member of the League precluded her from sending a note on the lines suggested. He also pointed out that Mr. Stimson made no complaint about the British refusal to write a similar note, but that he had complained—and with good reason—of the Foreign

Office *communiqué* to which Mr. Gull had referred. He went on to explain that the Foreign Office had never attempted to defend this *communiqué* and had always regretted that a slip had been made. In short, the case, as authoritatively put by a former official of the Foreign Office, was that there was an unfortunate act of *maladresse,* no unfriendly intention, but a conviction that it was the Government's duty to act through the League and not to take individual action in advance of joint action as a Member of the League.

It will perhaps be a fair summing-up of the British attitude regarding the Manchurian dispute to say that His Majesty's Government were unremitting in their endeavor to sustain, in collaboration with their fellow-members of the League and co-signatories of the Washington treaties and peace-pacts, the principles of peaceable settlement and of opposition to "aggression" with one qualification. The qualification was that they were not prepared to risk being left to bear the brunt of a war of retaliation by Japan, just as the United States, as Mr. Stimson clearly indicates in *The Far Eastern Crisis,* were themselves unprepared to resort to coercive measures such as economic sanctions or military pressure.[5] British policy was, in fact, based, as Sir John Simon told the House of Commons on March 22, 1932, on carrying out the policy and purposes of the League of Nations and on cooperation with other Powers; but in supporting the League it considered it best to "keep the coercive and the mediatory functions of the League distinct." There was a "dotting of the i's" in a further speech which the Foreign Secretary made about one year later, on February 27, 1933, after the final effort at conciliation by the League had failed. Sir John Simon then informed the House that "in no circumstances will this Government authorize this country to be a party to the struggle." This was the common attitude of the Powers which would have had to do the actual fighting in the event of war with Japan, and as Japan proved to be unsusceptible to moral pressure, the attempts to put international restraint on her over the Manchurian question now more or less petered out.

When, in March 1933 Japan gave notice of withdrawal from the League, the latter abandoned the endeavor to apply the principles of the Covenant to the Far Eastern imbroglio and

[5] *The Far Eastern Crisis,* pp. 76, 80, and 84.

virtually stepped aside, leaving the situation to work itself out without outside intervention.

In the immediately following years, there was no state of open conflict between Japan and China, and no direct international issues arose. We can therefore pass over this period of comparative quiescence and go on to the resumption of general hostilities in July 1937, which was followed by China's appeal to the League under Articles 11 and 17 of the Covenant. We need only observe in regard to the interval that during this time British Government spokesmen repeated at intervals the assurance that Great Britain would not recognize changes imposed by force, and would uphold the validity of the treaties between Great Britain and China, no modification of which could, they claimed, be accomplished except by negotiation between the principal parties. At the same time, the British Government endeavored, wherever possible, to promote direct settlements between China and Japan.

When the Sino-Japanese conflict again demanded decisions by the League Powers in the autumn of 1937, the attitude of the British Government was in essence similar to their attitude at the time of the Manchurian Affair, that is to say they still desired to make use of the—now much impaired—"collective" machinery, but for the purpose only of friendly mediation between the parties to the conflict. All suggestions of sanctions, or coercive action of any sort, such as were advocated by the Opposition parties in Parliament, were rejected, and for the same reasons as before. The Government declared that what they wanted to see brought about was a general Far Eastern settlement, but it must be a settlement by agreement between the principals. Friendly relations with both sides was, the Prime Minister stated, the aim of the British Cabinet. "Peace by agreement" was his watchword and this was the port towards which the British representatives steered in the part which they took in the League discussions at Geneva and, subsequently, at the Brussels Conference. At the end of 1937, however, the Prime Minister admitted by implication the hopelessness of working for an agreed peace. In a review of the development of the situation which he gave to the House of Commons on December 21 he said that "there was only one way in which the conflict could have been brought to an end . . . and that was not by peace but by force."

This attitude of the British Government in 1937 must be looked at in its relation to the international background, which had changed since the time of the Manchurian Affair. The League as a source of collective action had become an extremely weak reed, while, with tension growing in Europe, the United States more than ever held the key postion in any question involving the possible use of force in the Pacific, and the possibility of checking Japanese aggression depended to an increased extent upon the action which it might be possible for America to take. During the past few years there had been a marked growth of isolationist sentiment in America which could be attributed partly to the serious deterioration in the general international situation, and partly also to the American reaction to the incident of the supposed rebuff to Mr. Stimson in January 1932, which had wrongly induced the belief that Great Britain had refused to "go along" with America over the Manchurian affair. It was urgently important to dispel any misapprehension which might hinder Great Britain and the United States from working in harmony in face of the new crisis. When, therefore, China appealed once more to the League, the British Government's first step was to make it perfectly clear that, whatever action America might see fit to take, Great Britain, despite the European situation, would stand alongside her and take exactly the same action. In an apt and picturesque phrase Mr. Eden expressed this intention by saying that in order to secure American cooperation, he would be ready to fly not only from London to Geneva but from Melbourne to Alaska.

The next practical step was to remove the consideration of the measures to be taken in the Far East from the League to a conference of the parties to the Nine-Power Treaty in order that America might be represented by a delegate empowered to take an active part in the proceedings and publicly to declare his Government's policy. Before the meeting of this conference at Brussels, President Roosevelt had made his famous Chicago speech of October 5, in which he suggested that aggressor nations might be put in quarantine, but it was soon all too apparent that public opinion in America was in 1937 even more strongly opposed than it had been in 1931 to any action which might lead to entanglement in the affairs of other nations.[6] So

[6] For a statement of American reactions to the Chicago speech see the *Survey of International Affairs,* 1937, Vol. I, pp. 276 ff.

it came about that the American delegate came to Brussels with instructions to seek a solution by "peaceful processes." This for all practical purposes sealed the fate of the conference discussions. Unable to accomplish anything effective within the narrow confines set by Washington, it adjourned *sine die* after passing a resolution, subsequently adopted by the Assembly, which marked the limit beyond which the League Powers were not prepared to go. The resolution was that "Members of the League should refrain from taking any action which might have the effect of weakening China's powers of resistance, and should also consider how far they can individually extend aid to China." Collective action had been seen to hold such dangers that, while it was agreed that China ought to be helped, aid was only provided for on an individual basis.

If these developments in the autumn of 1937 had done nothing else, they had at least heavily underlined the fact expressed by the British Prime Minister in a speech at the Guildhall on November 9, 1937, that "an essential factor for success in any endeavor to bring about a settlement is the cooperation of the U.S.A."

However anxious the Government might be to take up the same position as America, there was no escape from the fundamental difficulty that, partly on account of the European situation and partly on account of the nature of her interests in the Far East, Great Britain was far more vulnerable to attack than America. The Japanese were fully aware of this fact and throughout the period took every available opportunity in ostentatiously meting out much more cavalier treatment to British than to American nationals and interests. By this policy they hoped to drive a wedge between Great Britain and the United States, and never quite lost the hope of reaching some kind of agreement with the latter. They seized on any American official statements suggestive of American dislike of overseas commitments such as Mr. Hull's description of United States policy given on January 10, 1938, namely that the Government in Washington "has asked, and is asking, that the rights of the United States and the rights of our people be respected, and at the same time it has sought and is seeking to avoid involvement of this country in the disputes of other countries." Moreover, the fact that Japan drew a large proportion of her supplies of essential war materials from America gave at this period a strong incentive to Japan to remain on friendly terms with the U.S. Government, but little similar motive for conciliating Great Britain.

While Great Britain was thus held up in Japan, sincerely or otherwise, as the chief obstacle to the realization of Japanese ambitions in China, and had focussed upon her a violent press campaign against foreign assistance to the Chinese, the Government at Washington was inhibited by the doctrine of non-involvement from action which might be interpreted by public opinion in America as taking a stand alongside Great Britain and relieving her of part of the brunt of the Japanese attack. It happened on two occasions, at least, when Great Britain was pressed particularly hard by Japan and stood in imminent danger of a deliberate attack, that the greatly needed support of an American *démarche* against Japan came just too late to serve as backing for British resistance to the demands being made by Japan. One such occasion was during the Tientsin negotiations, referred to below, when, after a "rearguard action" lasting for many months, the British Government concurred in the Craigie-Arita formula, which evoked wide criticism as being a near approach to the recognition of Japanese belligerent rights in North China which Japan was seeking to exact. The formula was announced on July 24, 1939. It was two days later, i.e., on July 26, that the American Government gave Japan warning of their intention to terminate their commercial treaty with her. Another similar case of unfortunate timing—unfortunate, that is, from the point of view of a British Government eminently dependent on American cooperation—was that of the Burma Road, which also will be dealt with more fully hereafter. The agreement to close the road, as Japan was demanding, was made public on July 18, 1940. It was a week after this date that President Roosevelt announced American restrictions fatal to the import by Japan of American supplies of essential war materials. It seems very probable that the British stand against Japan's demands could have been successfully maintained if the American Government could have acted before, and not after the critical junctures.

We must now turn to the more specifically British reactions to the Japanese menace, that is to say to action taken by Great Britain in her capacity as an individual State rather than that of a corporate Member of the League, or as a signatory to multilateral peace treaties. To do this we must retrace our steps by a few years and go back to 1935.

On July 11 of that year Sir Samuel Hoare, in a speech in the House of Commons, declared that "the maintenance of the principle of the Open Door coupled with full recognition of China's right to control her own destinies, remains the broad basis of British policy in China." This was the policy that had been enunciated in the "Chamberlain Memorandum" of December 1926, and though it conflicted with the Japanese claim of hegemony and of the right of veto over China's freedom to draw assistance from foreign sources, it was pursued with undiminished vigor. The most important measure taken in pursuance of this policy was the despatch of the Leith-Ross mission to the Far East in 1935. The occasion for this step was the American silver purchase policy which had been adopted the year before. This was, in the words of the author of the *Survey of International Affairs* for 1934, "doubly disastrous to China; it directly depleted her money reserves and her supply of coin in circulation, and it caused a violent appreciation of her currency on the foreign exchange market with all its adverse consequences for her external trade." The British Government proposed that the signatories of the Nine-Power Treaty should collaborate to avert the threatened disaster in China. In the spring of 1935 it was decided to send Sir Frederick Leith-Ross, Chief Economic Adviser to H. M. Government, on a mission to the Far East to investigate how such collaboration could be made effective. None of the Powers invited responded, however, to the suggestion of parallel action. In Japan the invitation to return to the path of collaboration envisaged in the Nine-Power Treaty was represented as a direct challenge to Japanese interests, and the arrival of the Leith-Ross mission in September 1935 was the signal for an outburst of suspicion and ill feeling. Eventually China solved her currency problem without the assistance of an international loan. On their own initiative the Chinese Government issued a decree nationalizing silver and establishing an inconvertible paper currency. The British Government, by simultaneously issuing an Order-in-Council making the decree binding upon British subjects and British institutions, was able to contribute towards the success of the new currency law. The reform of the currency was followed by an immediate revival of trade and industry, and for the first time for many years China was able to seek fresh capital abroad for industrial development. This movement the British Government stimulated both in the interest of trade and because they believed that China's economic regeneration offered one of the chief bulwarks against Japanese encroachment on her integrity. They encouraged the writing-off of old railway loans in default, the making of fresh loans for railway construction and other large-scale enterprises and extended the Export Credits Guarantee scheme to China. Great Britain had thus been making a substantial contribution towards helping China along the high road to prosperity when progress was cut short by the renewal of Japanese aggression on a large scale on July 7, 1937.

One of China's most crying needs now became munitions. Of these, Great Britain, having just embarked on a great rearmament program, had little to spare. Hongkong, however, was an important entrepôt for the supply of arms from all sources, and until Canton and the Canton-Kowloon railway fell into Japanese hands the British Government, in spite of Japanese threats and protests, refused to stop the transport of arms through Hongkong to China.

Considerable help was also given in improving communications between Burma and Yunnan. The British Government financed that section of the projected Burma-Yunnan railway which ran from Lashio to the Chinese frontier, while the Burma Government incurred considerable expenditure in improving their road system to carry the additional Chinese traffic and in building new roads to connect with the Burma-China highway. The Governments of Burma and India also gave facilities for the manufacture and assembly of aircraft destined for China and for the training of pilots, while the British and Chinese governments cooperated in the establishment of air services connecting India and Burma with China.

In 1938 China's currency problem had again become acute as the result of the conflict with Japan. In regard to a Government loan to China to relieve her financial difficulties, the British Government proceeded for a time with considerable caution. They would, they said, view favorably, and probably give their sanction to, any proposals for private British loans or long-term credits, but they could not grant a Government guarantee for a British loan to China (as they had done in the case of Turkey) because of the difficulties inherent in the fact that China was engaged in hostilities.[7]

This attitude accorded with Government statements in this earlier stage of the Sino-Japanese conflict tended to emphasize the neutral position of Great Britain in the Sino-Japanese struggle as one between two countries with whom she continued to have correct diplomatic relations. In November 1938 Mr. Chamberlain described the Government's attitude towards the Far Eastern situation as consisting in the desire for friendly relations with both sides, and of anxious waiting for the day when their differences would be composed and they could again turn their attention to the development of their resources and national welfare.[8]

By the end of 1938, however, the Government were overcoming their hesitation concerning the lending of money to China, and a step forward was taken when arrangements were made for the British Export Credit Guarantee Department to grant credits to the amount of £3 million to finance exports to China. A more important measure of financial assistance took place in March 1939 when the British Government went to China's aid by establishing a currency stabilization fund of £10 million, one-half of which was provided by British banks under a British Government guarantee. The Japanese attempt to supplant the Chinese national currency with a new currency under their control was an important part of their plan for conquering China. The stabilization fund was directly aimed at defeating Japanese plans by strengthening the position of the Chinese Government and their determination to continue resistance. It was difficult, one may observe, for the Japanese to raise formal objections since the establishment of the fund could be represented as a measure for the encouragement of British trade.

To complete the record of financial assistance it may be added

[7] To this the Opposition objected that the state of hostilities in China was itself the chief argument for British financial help in view of the resolution of the Powers represented at the Brussels Conference to extend to China all the assistance which they could give.

[8] Cf. Mr. Norman Davis's statement at the Brussels Conference that "We believe that cooperation between Japan and China is essential to the best interests of these two countries and to peace throughout the world." The assurance of the British Government's readiness to mediate at any favorable opportunity found place in the Speech from the Throne at the opening of Parliament on November 8, 1938.

at this point that a further £5 million was granted to the stabilization fund in December 1940, and a credit of £5 million for use
in the sterling area in June 1941; and, finally, in 1942 the
British Government undertook to make a loan of £50 million
upon terms to be agreed upon between the two Governments,
the details of which are at the time of writing (August 1942)
still under negotiation, the funds having, however, already
been made available for certain purposes. Besides these purely
financial forms of assistance, the British Government undertook
in February 1942 to make available for China under lend-lease
arrangements all the munitions and military equipment which
it is possible for Great Britain to supply.

British help to China during the period under review was,
of course, not solely material. In the memorandum of December 1926, the British Government had promised to relieve
China of the irksome burden of tutelage and to cooperate with
her in removing the shackles of the "unequal treaties." In
several important matters action had been taken to redeem this
promise and the major problems of extraterritoriality and the
"unequal treaties" would almost certainly have been disposed
of if discussions had not been stopped by the Japanese attack
on Manchuria. This circumstance was referred to in the British
Note to Japan of January 14, 1939, mentioned on a later page.
The Japanese Government were reminded that the negotiations
for the abolition of extraterritoriality had been interrupted by
the Manchurian conflict, but that H. M. Government have
always been ready to resume negotiations at a suitable time
and are prepared to discuss this and other similar questions
with a fully independent China when peace has been restored.
Later, on July 18, 1940 the Prime Minister made the following
statement on the subject in the House of Commons:—

"We wish for no quarrel with any nation in the Far East. We desire
to see China's status and integrity preserved, and as indicated in our note
of January 14, 1939, we are ready to negotiate with the Chinese Government after the conclusion of peace, the abolition of extraterritorial rights,
the rendition of concessions and the revision of treaties on a basis of
reciprocity and equality."

This was an occasion for parallel Anglo-American action.
Following the lead given by Great Britain the American Acting
Secretary of State declared on the following day that the United

States were ready to move in the same direction "whenever
conditions warrant."

Having seen how the British Government dealt firstly with
the threat from Japan to the peace machinery of the League,
and secondly with that to China's existence as a sovereign State,
we must now briefly examine what was done to meet the more
direct challenges to Great Britain's specific interests in the Far
East, and particularly her commercial stake in China. For the
defense of these interests the British Government took their
stand, in principle on the Nine-Power Treaty, refusing reso-
lutely to subscribe to the Japanese thesis that the régime established by the Treaty had been or should be, superseded by a
"new order" in East Asia.

The forms of threat to British vested rights in China were too
many to enumerate in detail. The most important were the following: the encouragement of large-scale smuggling of merchandise for the China market; the institution of Japanese-
controlled monopolies; the manipulation, under Japanese
auspices, of the Customs tariff and currency in North China;
obstruction to the movement of goods, especially to the ports;
the closure of inland waters to shipping, and interference with
the economic and administrative life of the foreign Settlement
and Concessions (Shanghai, Tientsin, and Canton) and of such
international services as River Conservancy Boards. To describe
seriatim the British Government's response to all these various
encroachments on foreign rights as well as to specific attacks
upon British lives and property (such as the bombing of the
British Ambassador and of British ships on the Yangtze) would
involve a tedious recital of diplomatic exchanges which would
add but little to the understanding of British policy, since it
was the general practice of the British Foreign Office to handle
each individual case on its own merits. It will suffice, therefore,
to give merely an indication of the broad line which the British
Government adopted in respect to each set of issues.

Against the activities of Japanese smugglers in China, Great
Britain protested (as did the United States) on the ground of
the prejudice to foreign trade competitors and the subversive
effects on the Chinese Maritime Customs service of wholesale
smuggling with Japanese support. In regard to the Customs
administration itself, the British Government demanded to be
consulted before the Japanese made any alterations in regard

to administration or to the disposal of revenues under Japanese *de facto* control.[9] The obstruction to British commercial activity at the ports, especially Shanghai and Tsingtao, was the subject of numerous representations by the British authorities, while a special protest in strong terms was made in November 1938 against the closure of the Yangtze to non-Japanese mercantile shipping. Questions arising out of Japanese interference with, and demands upon, the administration of the Shanghai International Settlement were recognized as being matters for arrangement primarily between the Japanese authorities and the Municipal Council. It was explained, however, in statements in Parliament that the British Government, while recognizing up to a point, the force in the Japanese claim for a larger measure of participation in the Shanghai administration (as distinct from representation on the Council), were in agreement with other Treaty Powers that the Municipal Council should be supported in resisting any attempts to interfere with their functions or to alter the character of the administration.

Another side of the challenge to British interests set out at the beginning of this section was the disturbance of the equilibrium of power in the Far East which was brought about by Japan's denunciation of the Naval Agreements, by her disregard of the Nine-Power Treaty (her signature to which had been the "indispensable guarantee that she would not abuse the regional immunity conferred upon her"[10] by the non-fortification provisions of the Washington Naval Treaty) and by her *rapprochement* to an aggressively minded Germany. The task of raising the level of Great Britain's defenses in the Far East to correspond to the new factors affecting British security occupied the Governments of Great Britain and of the British Dominions most closely concerned. Besides the general strengthening of the British combatant forces which came with the introduction of the "rearmament" policy in 1935, a speeding-up took place in the construction of the Singapore naval and air

[9] Subsequently the Government gave their concurrence to arrangements proposed by the Japanese Government for the servicing of the loans, but the scheme having failed to receive the necessary acquiescence of the Chinese Government, it remained inoperative.

[10] A. J. Toynbee: *Survey of International Affairs,* 1932, Oxford University Press, 1933.

bases, so as to make them available for general use in 1939;
Hongkong's defenses were improved, and plans were developed
for strategical cooperation with Australia and New Zealand.
When a possible threat to British security in Far Eastern waters
showed itself in the reported intention of the Japanese forces
to occupy the island of Hainan, the British Government concerted with the French Government in intimating to the Government of Japan that the occupation of the island would be calculated to arouse undesirable complications, and that such a
situation, if it arose, would call for consultation between Great
Britain and France as to the measures to be taken. In February
1939 the Japanese carried out their threat and the occupation
of Hainan began. The British Government, as well as the French
and United States Government, then made representations to
the Japanese Government and in reply received an assurance
that the occupation of the island was a temporary expedient
dictated by military necessity. At this point the matter was
allowed to rest.

On March 30, 1939, the Japanese Government who, as is now
evident, were already beginning to shape up for a conflict with
the Western Democratic Powers, announced the annexation by
Japan of Spratley Island (situated half-way between French
Indo-China and Borneo) over which France claimed jurisdiction. The British Under-Secretary of State for Foreign Affairs,
in reply to questions in the House of Commons as to the British
Government's intentions, admitted the great strategical importance of the island, but said that the question of protesing against
its annexation was one primarily for the French Government,
with whom "His Majesty's Government intend to keep in touch
in this as in all other matters of common concern." On June 22
a conference on the coordination of British and French strategy
in the Far East opened at Singapore. It was attended by nearly
fifty senior British and French naval, military, and air representatives from Indo-China, Hongkong, Shanghai, India, Burma,
Ceylon, Malaya, and Australia.

Specific Japanese challenges to British interests and principles of policy in the Far East found themselves merged, as has
already been said, in the all-embracing claim which Japan was
now making to the right to set up a "new order" bloc and a
"co-prosperity" zone (to use the phrase which later became
fashionable in Japan) in East Asia. The reiteration of this claim,

notably in Prince Konoye's public statements of November 3 and December 22, 1938, led the British Government to record their emphatic opposition to the Japanese plan. On December 7 Lord Plymouth told the House of Lords that His Majesty's Government "could not possibly subscribe" to a plan which, if carried out, "would inevitably have incalculable repercussions in other parts of the world, the consequences of which it would be impossible to limit." Some weeks later, on January 14, 1939, the British Government, following close on the footsteps of the United States Government, warned the Government in Tokyo that they could not accept the changes which it was the declared Japanese intention to bring about, and which implied the forcible compulsion of the Chinese to surrender their political, economic, and cultural life to Japanese control. H. M. Government, it was added, adhered to the principles of the Nine-Power Treaty and could not agree to its unilateral alteration, though they were always ready to consider constructive proposals put forward for treaty modification. Thus issue was unequivocally taken with Japan over the "new order."

Meanwhile at Tientsin a situation was developing which, inasmuch as it became in the sequel an important touchstone of British policy, calls for special attention. The details of the dispute between the local Japanese military and the British authorities need not be repeated;[11] its original substance consisted of Japanese grievances concerning the alleged inadequacy of the measures taken to prevent the British concession from being used by the Chinese as a base for anti-Japanese activities and of Japanese demands of assistance in imposing the "puppet" currency and in obtaining the surrender by Chinese banks in the Concession of part of the silver reserves of the national currency; to enforce their demands the Japanese Military blockaded the Concession and subjected British (and other foreign) nationals to intolerable indignities.

It soon became clear that, in the Japanese view, this was not a mere local issue but that the military, at all events, meant to use it as a side-door for achieving their aim of forcing Great Britain to abandon support for Free China and to "cooperate" in Japanese plans for imposing the "new order."

[11] See e.g., the accounts in China & Japan, Chatham House Information Papers, No. 21A, Part II, VI and I. S. Friedman: British Relations with China, 1931-39, IPR Inquiry Series, Institute of Pacific Relations, 1940, Chapter X.

That the Japanese should harbor such a hope was less strange in view of the patent fact that, with the war-clouds piling up in Europe, Great Britain had a strong incentive to do everything possible to avoid trouble in the Far East, the more so in view of the fact, which was probably not overlooked in Tokyo, that the British Government could not obtain a firm guarantee of American armed support in the last extremity owing to Washington's lack of constitutional powers to pledge the country to war without the consent of Congress.

H. M. Government recognized from the outset that major principles were at stake. A Foreign Office *communiqué* issued on June 16, 1939, put the position bluntly. Japan's demand for Great Britain's cooperation in the "new order" by renouncing her "pro-Chiang Kai-shek" policies would, it said, mean the abandonment under threats of force of the policy which H. M. Government has followed in the past . . . ," and it went on to give the warning that if Japan persisted, and refused to localize the incident, "an extremely serious situation will arise and the British Government will have to consider what immediate and active steps it can take for the protection of British interests in China." Having thus served notice that, in the final resort, Japan's challenge would be met, the British Government proceeded to use every endeavor to prevent the Tientsin affair from developing into an irrevocable clash. An appeal was made to the moderate feeling which, to outward appearance at least, was still a force in Japan. "I hesitate to believe," said the Secretary of State for Foreign Affairs in a public speech on June 21, "that the Government of Tokyo would wish deliberately to challenge the whole tradition and policy of Britain. I believe rather that a situation has developed out of some misunderstanding. . . ."

These complementary statements gave the keynote to the British Government's handling of the whole Tientsin affair and, indeed, of their policy up to the end of the period under review in the present section of this study. They never stirred from their position of refusal to compromise on essentials, that is on the basic principles of British policy, but, having their eyes on the growing menace in Europe, they were not going to risk a conflagration in the Far East brought about by causes of friction of a secondary nature; nor, if they could possibly prevent it, would they let Great Britain be manoeuvred into a position where she would have to bear the whole brunt, for a time at least, of Japanese military aggression.

It was in accord with this policy that the British Government acquiesced in the Japanese Government's desire for an agreed statement on the "background" of the dispute. This took shape in the "Craigie-Arita formula" of July 24, by which H. M. Government in the United Kingdom (i.e., omitting the Dominions overseas) recognized the "actual situation in China," admitted the special needs of the Japanese forces in respect to the safeguarding of their own security and the maintenance of public order in the regions under their control, and undertook not to countenance acts prejudicial to these needs. The formula was, as Mr. Chamberlain said on July 31, a statement of fact, denoting no change in British policy, which, he added, "this Government will not reverse at the request of another Power."

That the Tientsin negotiations subsequently hung fire was due, in the first instance, to Great Britain's stand on the third policy maxim mentioned just above, namely, determination not to be jockeyed into a position of isolation from her friends and associates. When the currency issue came on to the table the Japanese Government were told that no economic discussions could lead to useful results on a purely Anglo-Japanese basis, and that the views of interested third parties, i. e., the Nine-Power and other Treaty Powers, must be consulted. This the Japanese Government said that they "would never admit," and a deadlock ensued which put an end to the negotiations and deferred the final settlement for nearly a year, during most of which time the blockade of the British Concession and the anti-British campaign in North China continued unabated.

The United States Government's announcement, on July 26 of their intention to denounce the American trade treaty with Japan has already been mentioned, and the effect of the chronological sequence of events commented upon. It was perhaps inevitable that invidious comparisons between British and American action should have been drawn, especially by critics whose circle of vision was mainly confined to the Far Eastern stage and who failed to see it in perspective with the critical situation existing in the world as a whole. These critics were answered by Mr. Chamberlain in a speech in Parliament on August 4, 1939, when he pointed out the practical limitations under which Great Britain stood. "At the present time," he said, "we have not in the Far East a fleet superior to that of the Japanese. We have such a fleet here and in certain circumstances we may find it necessary to send that fleet out there." The first was a hard and inescapable fact, the relevancy of which was destined to be proved only too tragically two and a half years later; the second part of the statement was no doubt meant as a warning for Japan, but the well-informed among the Prime Minister's hearers can have had few illusions, even at that date, as to the chances of the British fleet being able to be spared from home waters in order to deal with the Japanese if things were brought to a crisis. Already the position had grown critical for the Japanese military were demonstrating at Tientsin, Kulangsu and Swatow, their readiness to resort to forcible measures against British establishments, and a further intimation was forthcoming in the blockade of Hongkong's Leased Territory which took place a little later. In Japan, Great Britain had become the "number one enemy."

Enough has been said to show the significance of the Tientsin negotiations as a touchstone of British policy; it remains to mention here (at the expense of overstepping the chronological limits of the section) the nature of the agreement which was finally reached on June 12, 1940. It proved a compromise which, on the one side, largely satisfied the Japanese demands for cooperation in suppressing terrorist activities against Japan and her "puppets," and, on the other hand, went a considerable way, in regard to the vexed questions of the rival currencies and the fate of the silver stocks, towards upholding the rights and interests of the Chungking Government, whose tacit acquiescence, if not vocal approval, Great Britain had made a *sine quâ non* in coming to a settlement.

2.   *The Last Phase:*

The start of the European war has, for convenience sake, been made the dividing point between the sections of this chapter, and it may be useful at this stage to sum up the main features of Great Britain's policy as displayed during the eight years which had elapsed since the Manchurian Affair up to September 1939. They may be set out under five headings:

(1) Determination on the part of the British Government to "take their full share in the carrying out of international obligations," while stopping short of warlike measures, or of such

other coercive action, as would be likely to lead to an armed conflict with Japan without a firm guarantee of outside assistance for Great Britain;

(2) British support for China in her struggle for independence within the limits set by the condition just mentioned and by the British Government's unwillingness to break off all amicable intercourse with Japan;

(3) Refusal to compromise the fundamental treaty basis of British rights in China, or to barter away principles in return merely for the restitution of violated rights, combined with a general tactical willingness to negotiate on individual issues;

(4) Readiness "to do everything honorably possible for peace"; and lastly,

(5) The desire for cooperation with the other Great Powers chiefly interested, i.e., the United States and France.

Actually, however, the outbreak of war in Europe was not an outstanding landmark in the record of British Far Eastern Policy, and after the Tientsin crisis which had reached its peak in the summer of 1939 the next milestone of major importance was the Burma Road dispute which occurred some ten months later. Before proceeding to deal with this a very brief survey may be made of developments during those months.

In the earlier stages there was a certain *détente* in Far Eastern affairs due to Japanese disgust at the German-Soviet pact and the Government's "independent" policy in relation to the European conflict. The policy included, however, increased concentration on the liquidation of the China Affair, which involved greater potentialities of friction with Great Britain as a supporter of Chinese independence. Consequently, in spite of the fact that several successive Japanese Governments apparently attempted to restrain the impatience of the military extremists and to keep on passable terms with the Democratic Powers, the situation did not fundamentally improve.

In these circumstances the British Government had no reason to modify their policy of inflexibility on major matters of principle tempered by pliancy in non-essential matters of dispute. This policy was illustrated in their treatment of the *Asama Maru* controversy at the beginning of 1940, which was adjusted on the basis of Great Britain releasing several of the Germans who had been seized on the Japanese ship as a concession to Japanese national feeling, and of Japan undertaking to cease carrying Germans returning homewards for national service. The Japanese Government's handling of the incident went some way to show that the British Government were justified in counting on moderating influences in Japan, capable, if encouraged, of putting the brake on the military extremists and so averting an immediate clash.

This hope grew fainter, however, as the year went on. The extremists, it became clear, were gaining ascendancy in Japan, and the collapse of Holland, and subsequently France, was rapidly opening fresh vistas of conquests to the eyes of the Japanese nation. In an attempt to circumscribe this dangerous growth of Japanese ambition, the British Government—acting again in unison with the United States but adopting the slightly lower key dictated by their more vulnerable position—entered a *caveat* against the Japanese pretensions in the Netherlands East Indies which were plainly implicit in the public statement made by Mr. Arita early in April concerning Japan's interest in the status of the Dutch possessions.

Similar British reactions to the onward march of Japan occurred in relation to China. Each fresh assault of importance on Chinese independence and sovereignty, such as the setting up of the Wang Ching-wei Government in Nanking in the spring of 1940, was met in London by the reiteration of Great Britain's unalterable intention to support China's independence and to treat the Chungking régime as the only legitimate Government. Chiang Kai-shek personally, too, commanded the unfailing trust and championship of the British public and Government in spite of whatever misgivings were felt from time to time concerning the visible weak points, economic and political, in China's internal structure, such as the failure to control price inflation and to effect any radical improvement in the relations between the Kuomintang and the Chinese Communists.

This being the fixed British attitude to China, H. M. Government found themselves in an extremely difficult dilemma when, in June 1940, the Japanese Government, having effectively stopped China from getting supplies through French Indo-China, turned their attention to the Burma Road, and demanded that its use for the transport of war material should cease. To realize the magnitude of the dilemma, one has to recall the state of affairs which existed at the end of June 1940. In the Far East the full weight of Japanese pressure was in process of being turned against Great Britain individually, and already the Japanese army was conducting a virtual blockade of Hongkong on the landward side. At home the British were in desperate straits. France had just fallen, the British Expeditionary Force, though it had escaped by the skin of its teeth, had lost nearly the whole of its equipment, and the threat of invasion hung heavily over the British Isles. Finally, but not least important, the amount of reliance which could safely be placed on American help in a head-on clash with Japan was particularly uncertain. The United States was just entering the throes of the presidential election and at such a time the Administration in Washington were bound to be especially cautious in committing themselves to anything in the nature of a warlike gesture such, for instance, as the despatch of American naval forces on a visit to Singapore, which in unofficial quarters was being advocated as a means of warning off Japan.

In these circumstances, H. M. Government—in what was to prove a forlorn hope—began by evading a categorical reply to Japan's demand for the closure of the road, contenting themselves with pointing out the difficulties in the way of accepting the Japanese suggestion and adverting to the fact that the Burma Road traffic would in any case automatically shrink with the coming rainy season. But the Japanese Government were not to be so easily put off. They expressed their "deep dissatisfaction" with this reply and requested its reconsideration.

The British Government were thus forced to a definite decision. Having, as the Prime Minister stated, taken into full consideration the attitude of America and Russia—and, by implication, having failed to discover therein sufficient encouragement to risk precipitating war—they gave a qualified acceptance to the Japanese demand and consented to close the road for three months to specified classes of war material.

The loud outcry which went up from many quarters both at home and abroad was answered by Mr. Churchill when he described the agreement in the House of Commons on July 18, the date of the road's closure. His explanation of the Government's motives and intentions was, in brief, as follows. The Government were not unmindful of their accepted obligations, including those to China; but they had also to consider that Great Britain was in the midst of a life-and-death struggle. It had been their aim to see a free and independent China, but at the same time they had wanted to improve relations with Japan. To gain this double goal time was needed and respite from tension. Relief of tension depended on paying attention to Japan's complaint about supplies to China; the gaining of time could be accomplished by making a *temporary* arrangement, and the time so gained might, the Government hoped, be used to promote a just and equitable solution of the Sino-Japanese conflict "freely accepted by both."

It is clear that the decision to close the Road was based primarily upon military considerations. In the light of experience there can be little doubt that the decision was justified by the circumstances which prevailed. It was widely believed, even by Great Britain's friends, that the fall of France would be followed by the speedy defeat or surrender of Great Britain. The Japanese were elated at the prospect and a straight refusal then would almost certainly have led to an immediate attack—not on Great Britain and America—but on Great Britain alone. At that moment such an attack might have spelled defeat. By temporizing three precious months were gained during which this country rearmed and prepared for a long war, and at the end of which the Battle of Britain had been won. The elation in Japan died down and when the Road was reopened hardly a murmur was raised.

In the three months during which the Burma Road was closed there occurred two events which greatly influenced the current trend of British policy towards Japan. The first was the compulsion put by Japan on French Indo-China to admit Japanese garrison troops in Tongking; the second was the signature of the Three-Power Pact. The former was a manifest move in the direction of Japanese domination of the French colony. In regard to adjacent territories its immediate threat was against China, but, taken in conjunction with other symptoms such as Japan's political manoeuvres in Siam, it made it appear more than likely that the "southward thrust" was imminent. The latter event, the signing of the Pact, left no doubt that Japan was ranging herself irrevocably on the side of our opponents in the world war.

The effect of these two events undoubtedly was to stiffen the British attitude to Japan. The Government could not but feel that the prospect of restraining Japan by making concessions had very greatly diminished, and that increased reliance must be placed on showing the Japanese that further provocative action would be met with counter-action by the Western Democracies and would lead eventually to war.

It was in this setting that Mr. Churchill announced the Government's decision to reopen the road on October 17. He recalled that, in acceding to Japan's demand for its closure, the Government had hoped to furnish an opportunity for Japan and China to reach a just and equitable settlement. Japan had made no such attempt; she had instead, the Prime Minister pointed out, made a pact with the Axis Powers, a pact aimed primarily against the United States.

The hardening trend given to British—and to American— policy by Japan's entry into the Axis and her unmistakable designs upon the countries of southeast Asia continued, with gathering force, from the time of the reopening of the Burma Road to the outbreak of the war in the Pacific on December 7, 1941. Apart from this there is comparatively little more that needs to be said about the development of British policy in the Far East during those fourteen months. It was now progressing along clearly defined lines and the only question was that of tempo. This was regulated primarily, of course by Japanese actions, and secondly, in the main, by the United States, in virtue of the fact that she possessed by far the stronger forces available in the Pacific as backing for Anglo-American common policy.

In this connection Great Britain suffered throughout from the inevitable disadvantage of having no positive guarantee of American assistance in defending British, or Dutch, territory in the event of an attack by Japan. The United States Government had no constitutional power to pledge the country to war, and consideration had also to be given to the fact that there still existed in America a substantial body of opinion opposed to involvement in hostilities in any part of the world. As, however, the concrete signs of American determination—such as the disposition of her fleets, oil-embargoes, et cetera—multiplied, so Great Britain was enabled to exert correspondingly greater pressure on Japan and open support for China. The first took the form of repeated warnings and of progressive economic restrictions, while China was helped by additional economic support, facilities for aircraft production in neighboring British territory, and closer military liaison.

The economic pressure on Japan reached its high point in July 1941 when, in open reprisal for Japan's enforcement of her military claims on Indo-China, the British Government denounced the Anglo-Japanese trade treaties and joined with the United States and the Netherlands Government in freezing Japanese assets.

These and other more localized measures against Japan, such as restrictions on the working of the important Japanese-owned iron-ore mines in Malaya, were calculated to leave Japan in no possible doubt of the determination of Great Britain, together with her associates, to set a near limit to Japanese aggression. Nevertheless the British Government showed their desire up to the last to leave a loophole for Japan in the slender hope that more moderate councils might still prevail and cause Japan to confine herself to the strictly pacific objectives which some of her statesmen persisted in declaring to be her sole aim. Thus Mr. Eden, when reviewing in Parliament the critical situation which had developed in July 1941, added to his indictment of Japanese action an appeal to such relics of statesmanship as might survive in Japan.

"It is," he said, "a matter of regret to His Majesty's Government that their relations with Japan should have reached their present state. But the fault does not lie with His Majesty's Government. Japan complains of encirclement. Yet it is Japan herself who, by successive acts of aggression, has drawn closer and closer together in self defence the countries which lie in her path and whose territories and interests are ever more sharply threatened. I cannot believe that statesmanship in Japan is entirely dead or blind; and I sincerely trust that those responsible for the destinies of the Japanese Empire will reflect, while there is yet time, whither their present policy is leading them."

As the prospect of a final breach with Japan came nearer, unity of action between the Governments of London and Washington became progressively more pronounced, and all important diplomatic moves were enacted à deux.

When, for instance, the State Department declared its readiness to negotiate, after peace, the surrender of extraterritorial rights in China, Mr. Eden seized the opportunity to restate the promises already previously given to China by His Majesty's Government, as mentioned earlier. In their note of January 14, 1939, the British Government had stated, as the reader may be reminded, that they had always been prepared to resume the negotiations for the abrogation of British extraterritorial rights, which had been allowed to lapse by the Chinese in 1931 after Japan's seizure of Manchuria, and that they were prepared to discuss this and other similar questions with a fully independent Chinese Government after the restoration of peace. Later, on July 18, 1940, the Prime Minister had repeated this pledge, reaffirming that when peace was restored His Majesty's Government were ready to negotiate with the Chinese Government the abolition of extraterritorial rights, the rendition of concessions, and the revision of treaties on the basis of reciprocity and equality.

That the "Washington conversations" were conducted without the participation of the British Government was due, it can safely be assumed, to no differences of general outlook between Washington and London, but rather to tactical motives or, it might be, to Japanese insistence upon dealing with America alone. The British Government were not uninformed of the development of the conversations and of the American Government's plan for a broad settlement of the problems of the Far East. This is clear from the summary given to Congress in which the President stated that "appropriate contact" was kept with the representatives of other countries whose rights and interests were involved.

It seems highly probable that the sole condition on which the Japanese were prepared seriously to try to negotiate a settlement was that China should be left to their tender mercies, and there can be no doubt whatever that the United States and British Governments were at one in refusing to contemplate any such betrayal of their common principles.

On September 9, 1941, shortly after his return from his meeting with President Roosevelt in the Atlantic, Mr. Churchill told the House of Commons that one of the main subjects discussed had been the policy to be pursued towards Japan in order, if possible, to put a stop to further encroachment in the Far East likely to endanger the safety or interests of Great Britain or the United States. At that time the course of the Japanese-American conversations was secret, but it was known that attempts were being made in Washingon to reach with the Japanese the basis for a comprehensive settlement of the whole Far Eastern problem on peaceful and equitable lines. That the attempt received the firm support of H. M. Government was put beyond doubt in Mr. Churchill's broadcast to the British nation of August 24, when, after describing Japan's career of aggression and declaring that "this has got to stop," he went on to say:

"The United States are labouring with infinite patience to arrive at a fair and amicable settlement which will give Japan the utmost reassurance for her legitimate interests. We earnestly hope these negotiations will succeed. But this I must say: that if these hopes should fail we shall of course range ourselves unhesitatingly at the side of the United States."

Three months later, Mr. Churchill repeated the pledge of solidarity with the United States in terms even more emphatic. In his Mansion House speech on November 10 he said:

"They (the United States) are doing their utmost to find ways of preserving peace in the Pacific. We do not know whether their efforts will be successful, but, should they fail, I take this occasion to say, and it is my duty to say, that, should the United States become involved in war with Japan, the British declaration will follow within the hour."

It was with a fresh reminder of this pledge that Mr. Churchill opened his speech to Parliament on December 8 announcing Great Britain's declaration of war on Japan in reply to Japanese attacks on British territory.

An analysis of British Far Eastern policy might appear incomplete if it contained no reference at all to post-war policy. The British Government having consistently held to the point of view that it is premature for them to formulate peace aims so long as the end of the war is hidden from view, there is, as a matter of fact, not much that can usefully be said on this subject. There has, however, been fairly widespread public discussion of the geographical scope of the Anglo-American Joint Declaration of August 14, 1941, known as the "Atlantic Charter," and it may be well to make mention of such British official statements as bear applicability of the "Charter" principles to the Far East and Pacific area.

Commenting on the Joint Declaration in his speech in the House of Commons on September 9, 1941, Mr. Churchill remarked that its authors had primarily in mind the future of the nations in Europe under the Nazi yoke, a quite separate problem, he remarked, from that of the progressive evolution of self-governing institutions in dependent territories. With regard to the latter—i. e., the development of self-government in regions owing allegiance to the British Crown—H. M. Government had, Mr. Churchill observed, made unambiguous declarations which were complete in themselves, though entirely in harmony with the conceptions which inspired the Joint Declaration. He was referring to statements of policy made from time to time about the development of constitutional Government in India, Burma and other parts of the British Empire and especially, no doubt, to the pledge given in August 1940 to help India along the road to free and equal partnership in the British Commonwealth.

Another aspect of this question, namely the appropriateness or otherwise to Japan's case of the principles which the Declaration establishes in regard to post-war relations with a defeated Germany, was touched upon in an earlier speech delivered at Coventry on August 30, 1941 by the Secretary of State for Foreign Affairs. Mr. Eden began by reminding his audience of his previous definition of British intentions towards Germany after the war. It consisted of two things. On the one hand Germany must be prevented from rearming and resuming the struggle for domination over peace-loving nations; on the other, she must not, as the result of economic collapse, become a source of poison to her neighbors and the world. "These two fundamental principles," Mr. Eden went on to say, "must govern not only our relations with Germany after the war, but all international relations. This is the plain meaning of the Roosevelt-Churchill Declaration. No nation must ever be in a position to wage aggressive war against her neighbors. And, secondly, economic relations must be so regulated that no nation can in future be starved out of its proper economic position by autarchic methods of trade arbitrarily imposed."

CHAPTER IV

CONCLUSION

From the early years when Lord Palmerston found it necessary to insist that the British merchant in China should respect Chinese institutions to the day when Mr. Churchill, in the course of summing up the situation at the outbreak of the present war with Japan, declared "China's cause is our cause," the preservation of Chinese independence has been the thread on which British policy in the Far East has been strung. The axiom that China should be free from the domination or tutelage of any Great Power has been at the root of Great Britain's relations with other countries concerned with the Far East, and has in large degree determined her international friendships and enmities in respect to that area.

When the threat has appeared to wear thin, as it has at certain junctures, this has been due not to a change of policy but to the unavoidable fact that Great Britain, as a European State and a world Power, has had to coordinate her actions in the Far East with her general policy vis-à-vis European neighbors, and ever and anon to subordinate the former to the latter. In this matter she has been far more trammeled than, for instance, the United States, her principal fellow-champion of Chinese independence, and correspondingly less free to follow out a specifically "Far Eastern" policy regardless of events in other parts of the world.

The motives which led Britain to make the principle of Chinese independence the pivot of her policy have been discussed at various points in the course of the previous chapters. By reviewing them very briefly against the changing scene of world developments over the century covered by the study the essential nature and unity of British Far Eastern policy may perhaps be made more clearly discernible.

British policy in the 19th century was at the start the handmaid of British trade, and only gradually changed from an almost purely commercial to a more political character. When established trading relations met with obstruction from the Central Government's officials, Britain resorted more than once to force in order to obtain what she regarded as tolerable conditions for her own—and indirectly for all nations'—commerce, but British statesmen held throughout, and acted on, the conviction that the interests of British trade required the existence of an effective central authority in China. The special rights acquired under the early treaties became, as is now evident, a factor in hastening the decline of the central authority. This, however, was largely obscured at the time, and sufficient proof of the British Government's standing desire to keep that authority intact can be shown by the single instance of the care with which its rights were upheld in the emergency arrangements made at Shanghai during the Taiping rebellion for collecting the Customs dues on behalf of an "absentee" Government.[1]

When, towards the end of last century, the dangers from without began to outstrip the dangers from within threatening the survival of China as an independent Power, Great Britain's policy of assisting her survival by preventing third-party domination crystallized even more clearly, and to no inconsiderable extent helped to determine the trend of the whole of British foreign policy during a particularly critical period. As the threat to dominate China came successively from one quarter or another, Great Britain ranged herself in turn against the potential aggressors and combined with those Powers including Japan which were best able to check their advance.

The defeat of Russia by Japan, the creation for a while of an equilibrium of forces throughout the world as a whole by means of the international groupings which took their start in the British-Japanese alliance, and the advent of the United States as a strong champion of the "open door" in China, reduced for a time the urgency of the problem of preserving China's independence. It revived in a more dangerous form when the First World War, by cancelling out the Great Powers of Europe for the time being, gave Japan her opportunity to aspire to hegemony in the Far East.

The implications of the new threat to China's integrity became fully apparent only after the Manchurian affair in 1931. In 1921, however, the writing on the wall had become sufficiently obvious to cause Great Britain to terminate her alliance

[1] See H. B. Morse: *International Relations of the Chinese Empire*, 3 vols., Longman's, 1910-18.

with a Power who was clearly becoming the chief menace to that doctrine of Chinese independence on which British policy was based, and which, on the instance of Great Britain and the United States, was made the central point of the Washington Nine Power Treaty.

Meanwhile the doctrine had acquired fresh significance for Great Britain, and new motives had been joined to those already existing for affording every support to China's efforts to set up a unified and stable government. In the first place the war had brought home the need for suppressing at the source potential causes of conflict, and there had been at the same time a more conscious and far-reaching development of the British instinctive feeling for the "rule of law." Hence it had come to be recognized that aggression *per se*—by any Power in any part of the world—was a matter of essential national concern and that its prevention must in future be a primary aim of British policy;[2] and associated with this, there was a sense of Great Britain's obligation to share in the collective safeguarding of national freedom and independence throughout the entire world. Secondly, taking a long view, the creation of a Japanese hegemony in the Far East involving the formation of a Sino-Japanese, or even an East Asian, *bloc,* would be liable to upset to an exceptional extent the general distribution of power throughout the world. Thirdly, the immediate strategic implications of another Power, especially if it were Japan, becoming able to use China and neighboring territories as a military base, had assumed vastly greater importance through the development of aviation and the much increased radius of military striking power, particularly as it had the effect of bringing Australia, New Zealand, and India well into the picture.

Lest it should be thought that excessive emphasis has here been given to China's independence as the objective of British policy, it may not be amiss to end with a reference to a document which, although composed three and a half decades ago, is universally held to be one of the most penetrating analyses of British foreign policy which has ever been written. In his confidential Foreign Office memorandum of January 1, 1907, Sir Eyre Crowe, later Permanent Under-Secretary of State, having

---

[2] The manner and extent to which circumstances elsewhere in the world weakened the hands of the British Government in giving effect to this policy on later occasions have been dealt with in the previous chapter.

pointed out Great Britain's particular need, as a world-wide maritime Power, to identify her national policy with the primary interests of as many other nations as possible, wrote:

"Now the first interest of all countries is the preservation of national independence. It follows that England, more than any other non-insular Power, has a direct and positive interest in the maintenance of the independence of nations and therefore must be the natural enemy of any country threatening the independence of others and the natural protector of the weaker communities."

If this view of British policy is correct, added Sir Eyre Crowe later in the same memorandum, then "the opposition into which England must inevitably be driven to any country aspiring to such a dictatorship assumes almost the form of a law of nature."

From July 1937, when the "China Incident" began, support for China's independence became to an ever-increasing extent an integral and vital part of the wider problem of checking Japan's aggressive designs on "East Asia" and of defending Great Britain's own Far Eastern possessions. Chapter III of this study shows how indissolubly the two were merged into each other. If it reveals at the same time the limits which military unpreparedness set to Great Britain's ability fully to implement her policy vis-à-vis China, the record also shows, notably in the case of the closing and reopening of the Burma Road, how ready the British Government were to realign their actions with their fundamental policy whenever the military risks were not reckoned to be prohibitive. In the last phase of all, Anglo-American refusal to "sell out" China to Japan was almost certainly the crucial factor in precipitating the war with Japan. According to General Tojo's statement to the Diet of November 17, 1941, "non-obstruction" in China was the first on the list of Japan's "demands" on the Democratic Powers, and its acceptance might have delayed the outbreak of the Far Eastern conflict for a considerable period. This eventuality was utterly precluded by the stand taken by the two Governments in support of China's independence.

In thus tying their policy to the principle of Chinese independence successive British Governments were, consciously or unconsciously, following the dictates of those fundamental national interests which the writer set out to define in the opening words of this study. The principle gave expressions to the ordinary Englishman's desire to see Great Britain free to trade overseas, the British Empire secure, and the world as a whole at peace, while at the same time it reflected that traditional attachment to, and respect for, liberty which at different times has ranged Englishmen on the side of Italian, Greek, Bulgarian and other fighters for freedom and which, in the sphere of colonial government, has led Great Britain to adopt as a guiding principle the evolution of self-government.

CHAPTER V

SUPPLEMENTARY CHAPTER

Developments after the outbreak of the Pacific war were touched upon lightly in the preceding chapters; they will now be looked at in greater detail.

Leaving out of account its more purely strategic aspects, British policy during this latest period has again been concerned principally with China—naturally so, not only because China was now the only Far Eastern State with which Great Britain remained in diplomatic relations, but also because of China's enhanced importance to the British Commonwealth as a fighting ally, a co-member of the family of United Nations, and an associate with Great Britain in the task of solving the problems of post-war settlement.

The primary concern of Great Britain, as of the United States, was to do everything possible to assure that China should, in spite of all difficulties and handicaps, maintain the common struggle against Japan, and for this purpose to keep her supplied with all possible material. The forms which earlier assistance took have already been specified in pages 49-51, and to the catalogue there given there is little to add. As the Japanese progressively advanced, aid to China became more and more a question of means of conveyance, requiring much enterprise and great boldness of conception on the part of the British Government and the Government of India in devising and organizing new routes through ever more difficult terrain to take the place of those successfully cut by the enemy. The tangible fruits of these efforts were necessarily meager, less valuable perhaps than the proof which they gave of Great Britain's determination to fulfil her promise to China to provide every aid in her power. Under lease-lend arrangement it fell to American transport planes, operating from British bases in India, to contribute the major share in conveying Allied supplies to China.

In the meantime British diplomacy in China was having to contend with adverse winds from divers points of the compass.

A marked lowering of regard for the white races had come about as a result of the initial disasters which befell the British and American armed forces in the Pacific. There was also a good deal of openly expressed Chinese dissatisfaction with the management of the operations in Burma, where complaints were made against the British military authorities of undue hesitancy in accepting Chinese offers of collaboration, and, finally, there was considerable impatience with the Anglo-American war effort as being too much directed against Germany and too little against Japan. Besides this back-lash of the reverses suffered in the war in the Pacific, there was the critical Chinese reaction to the conflict which developed in 1942 between Government and Congress in India. In the autumn of 1942 there was, in fact, much leeway to make up if Anglo-Chinese relations were to be restored to the footing of mutual trust and good-will which was essential to smooth and efficient cooperation both during and after the war.

The recovery of no small part of this leeway by the spring of 1943 was due, in large part, to the successful conclusion on January 11, 1943, of a treaty whereby Great Britain surrendered extra-territorial rights in China so that the relations between the two countries were placed on a basis of absolute equality.

The promises given to China up to July 1940 in regard to the relinquishment of special rights are recorded above in pages 51, 64-65. The principle having been conceded, the question of the time for implementation asserted itself. There were obvious advantages in waiting, as originally proposed, till after the defeat of Japan and the restoration of peace. The Japanese would then have been expelled from Chinese soil and China would be united, so that the changes to be made could take effect simultaneously throughout the entire country. After victory the Governments concerned would be free from the distraction and complications of war, and could more easily devote the necessary time and consideration to the working out of practical details. Perhaps, too, more grace might be felt to attach to a voluntary divestment of rights by Great Britain and America when they should have redeemed the position lost by their earlier defeats at the hand of the common enemy.

The case for immediate action could be summed up in the adage *bis dat quis cito dat,* and it was, no doubt, with this principle in mind that the British and American Governments, acting in unison, announced on October 10, 1942, their intention of inviting the Chinese Government to enter immediately into negotiations for the conclusion of treaties to give effect to their offer to relinquish their extra-territorial and cognate rights. The difficulty of settling forthwith the many complex arrangements necessitated by the transition from the old "treaty-port" régime to one of the modern type was at the same time met by proposing that further comprehensive treaties of commerce, navigation and consular rights should be negotiated at a later convenient time.

The British and American negotiations with China proceeded along parallel lines in Chungking and Washington respectively. They were virtually completed by the end of 1942 and signature took place simultaneously in the two national capitals on January 11, 1943. Thanks to close collaboration between the State Department and the Foreign Office, the two agreements are as nearly as possible identical on all common points. The territories to which the British treaty applies are the United Kingdom of Great Britain and Northern Ireland, India, and the British colonies and protectorates; but not the self-governing Dominions, who dealt with the matter independently. The treaty was signed by a separate plenipotentiary in respect of India. The negotiations aimed at complete equality and reciprocity between the signatory Powers and all rights and privileges which conflicted with this principle were relinquished. Among these the more important covered by the treaty and supplementary exchange of notes were (1) extra-territorial jurisdiction in China, (2) the rights derived from the 1901 (Boxer) protocol, including the stationing of troops in certain areas and participation in the control of the diplomatic quarter at Peking, (3) the British concessions at Tientsin and Canton and the administrative rights shared with other foreign Powers in the International Settlements at Shanghai and Amoy, (4) the special rights enjoyed by British naval vessels in Chinese waters and participation by British flag merchant shipping in the Chinese inland navigation and coastal trades.

For the renunciation of these various rights and privileges British interests received a certain concrete compensation in the form of the right, under the terms of the treaty, for British nationals to reside, trade, and trade anywhere in China, instead of being legally confined, as before, to specified areas. But what was of far greater value was the moral effect of the treaties upon Chinese opinion. They were acclaimed with the greatest enthusiasm as the instruments of China's long-awaited liberation from the stigma of unequal international status and as the opening of a new era full of promise for relations with the signatory countries.

There had been in Chungking some unofficial agitation for the return of Hongkong by Great Britain to China as part of the change to be made by the new treaty. The Chinese Government made no such proposition, but they did, as their Foreign Minister let it be known after the signature of the treaty, press for the cancellation of the lease of the Kowloon territories on the mainland. The view of the British Government on this point was, it was understood, that no connection existed between the lease[1] and the extra-territorial rights and special privileges which Great Britain was offering to give up, and that, furthermore, the Kowloon territory had so many and such close economic links with Hongkong that the life of the colony had become inseparably bound up with the existing régime on the mainland. The upshot was that the matter of Kowloon was not included in the treaty, but that the Chinese Government reserved the right to reopen the question for discussion with H.M. Government at a later opportunity.

The treaty for the surrender of extra-territoriality consummated a trend in British policy which had begun nearly a century earlier. It had been the wish throughout of the British Government to divest themselves of extra-territorial rights as soon as China should have brought her laws and judicial system nearly enough into line with those of the West. This intention was set out in Art. 12 of the Mackay Treaty of 1902, albeit with a somewhat vague saving reference to "other considerations" which might enter into account. At the Washington Conference the British Government joined in resolving to set up an International Commission to investigate the abolition of extra-territoriality, and they did so in the confident belief that this was a practical step towards the object in view. Four and a half years passed before the resolution was put into effect by sending a Commission to China. The responsibility for the delay lay principally with the French Government who were engaged in a long-drawn-out dispute with the Peking Govern-

---

[1] For particulars of this see above, page 24.

ment over the gold-franc issue which arose in connection with the service of French loans to China, but the other Governments signatory to the Washington Agreement can hardly be absolved from the charge of a certain inertia in the matter. When the Commission finally assembled in Peking in 1926, the state of governmental disorganization in China rendered its labors almost nugatory.

Meanwhile, however, the British Foreign Office had boldly decided on the principle of not making an improvement of conditions in China a necessary preliminary to progress towards treaty revision, and on December 18, 1926, Sir Austen Chamberlain had issued the epoch-making memorandum referred to on page 35. In the following year H.M. Government had advanced a further step by notifying the Chinese Government of their readiness to recognize the recently formed, modern-style Chinese Law Courts as competent to deal with actions by British plaintiffs, to apply within practical limits the modern Chinese civil code in the British Courts, and to make British subjects liable to Chinese non-discriminatory taxation. On December 20, 1929, they had informed the Government of China that they were willing to agree that the following New Year's Day should be treated as the date for commencing in principle the gradual abolition of extra-territoriality, as to which they submitted proposals concerning time-tables and conditions in November 1930, at the same time as the United States Government. In the following year they entered on hard business by opening the negotiations in Nanking which were conducted by Sir M. Lampson and Dr. C. T. Wang.

This short epitome will suffice to show how completely devoid of truth was the accusation voiced by Japanese propaganda at the time of the signing of the treaty of January 11th that the hands of the British and American Governments had been forced by events, and that they had acted against their own will. That this was untrue not only of the Government itself, but also of the major British mercantile interests concerned, is proved by the attitude adopted by the latter towards the Government's action in giving up special rights.

The China Association in London, which is comprehensively representative of the old established British firms doing business with China, put on record its attitude to the new treaty in a letter published in *The Times* of November 2, 1942. The letter referred to what had been written in *The Times* of October 22 by the newspaper's own correspondent in China about the British merchant and his standpoint. The British merchant, the writer had said, was asking "not for the dubious help of the outworn safeguards of the past, but for the promise of equal (i.e., equal for all) treatment in the future." This, said the Chairman of the China Association in his letter to the editor of *The Times*, was the attitude of the Association itself. "Its approval," he went on to say, "of our Government's attitude connotes a good deal more than acceptance without demur of an action so obviously necessary; it includes also a keen desire to work with China's businessmen on a footing of cordial and constructive reciprocity." No longer could it be said, in the light of such a declaration, that the British merchant was lagging behind his Government in giving practical recognition to the changes which time had brought about in the relationship between the foreign merchant and the people and Government of China.

Anglo-Chinese relations experienced a further improvement from the visit to China of a British Mission representing the two Houses of Parliament and containing members of each of the main political parties. The Chinese received the Mission most cordially, evincing a lively interest in the practical working of the British parliamentary system, an interest not perhaps unconnected with China's own impending problems of effecting the transition from the stage of "tutelage" to that of "full democratic" government in accordance with Dr. Sun Yat-sen's program of political evolution.

Political developments in India had, in the meantime, threatened to cloud the prospect for a good Sino-British understanding. Chinese opinion as voiced in the press, sides strongly with the Congress Party in its demand for the immediate transfer of power, largely ignoring the problem of religious and class differences with which the Government of India was faced, and tending to treat the Party as representing the mass of the people of India as a whole in the same way that the Kuomintang represents the people of China. The civil disobedience campaign was generally condoned, and the Government was criticized when it refused to surrender to violence. There was a good deal of unofficial advocacy of American intervention.

Generalissimo Chiang visited India and met there the principal political leaders. He afterwards sent a message to the people of India admonishing them to collaborate in the common struggle against Japan and the Axis. In the course of this message he made an appeal to Great Britain to lose as little time as possible in transferring "real political power" to Indians.

Though the Chinese authorities refrained from taking any action calculated to increase the difficulties of H.M. Government of India, there was an evident lack of sympathy for these difficulties and of appreciation of the sincere efforts of the Government—particularly in sending out the Cripps Mission —to expedite self-government for India as much as the communal problem and the needs of defense might permit.

Meanwhile, added to the new political bond, the vast practical importance to China which India had now assumed as the "bridge" for assistance and for contact with the West caused a great enhancement of Chinese interest in India, and a closer link was created between the two countries by the exchange for the first time of representatives, with the titles respectively of Chinese Commissioner in India and Agent-General of the Government of India in China.

British policy in India *per se* calls for no further attention in these pages, lying as it does outside the scope of this study.[2]

Great Britain's Colonial policy, on the other hand, cannot be omitted, for it is inseparably linked with British Far Eastern policy, and must remain so while Burma, Malaya, Hongkong, North Borneo and the enemy-occupied portions of the Pacific dependencies, though severed by the fortunes of war, continue to be thought of as part of the British Colonial Empire and of that wider entity, the British Commonwealth of Nations. There follows, therefore, a short appreciation of current British Colonial policy, with special reference to post-war settlement in the Far East.

H.M. Government has issued no formal declaration of Colonial policy during the present war. On December 3, 1942, they were asked in the House of Lords for a statement of Colonial policy in relation to the Atlantic Charter. On that occasion Lord Cranborne, as Colonial Secretary, said in reply that anything in the nature of a "Colonial Charter" could not but

[2] It has, moreover, been dealt with in another I.P.R.-sponsored publication, Sir Frederick Whyte's *India: A Bird's-Eye View*.

involve misleading over-simplification, since the diversification of the Colonial territories and constant evolution of the whole political organism made it impossible for H.M. Government to have a standardized policy. Though for an inquiry such as the present there is, therefore, no comprehensive Government pronouncement to serve as a guide, there is available a considerable body of ministerial statements made from time to time, and, in addition to these, a collection of unofficial but representative British views on Colonial policy formulated by members of the United Kingdom delegation to the Eighth I.P.R. Conference. These statements, from whatever points of the political compass they come, show a unanimity on certain main fundamentals which makes it possible to identify, provisionally at least, certain axioms as representative of British opinion and intention concerning the Colonies and their future.

The first of these is that the British Colonial Empire is not to be thought of as obsolescent, still less as in liquidation. It is, as Lord Cranborne said in the House of Lords debate mentioned above, not a thing which is coming to an end, but one which calls for work by the British people which is now only beginning. What might be called the classical exposition of this doctrine came from Mr. Churchill himself, couched in characteristic language, in his Mansion House speech of November 10, 1942. He was speaking of France's possessions in North Africa, and in this connection he said that Great Britain was free of any "acquisitive appetite" there, or elsewhere in the world, since, as he said, she was fighting not for profit but honor.

"Let me, however," he continued, "make this clear, in case there should be any mistake about it in any quarter. We mean to hold our own. (Loud cheers.) I have not become the King's First Minister in order to preside over the liquidation of the British Empire. (Loud cheers.) For that task, if ever it were prescribed, someone else would have to be found, and, under democracy, I suppose the nation would have to be consulted. I am proud to be a member of that vast commonwealth and society of nations and communities gathered in and around the ancient British monarchy, without which the good cause might well have perished from the face of the earth. Here we are, and here we stand, a veritable rock of salvation in this drifting world."

A Labour Minister, Mr. Herbert Morrison, speaking at Newcastle on January 10, 1943, expressed himself as definitely, if in less emphatic phraseology, about the desirability of the British Commonwealth (including, of course, the Colonies) continuing to exist "not because it is British, but because it is good."

These and parallel statements show the renascence of a sense of national responsibility in connection with the Colonial Empire, of faith in Great Britain's educative and standard-raising task, and of pride in the manner in which she has dealt and is dealing with those tasks. There are frequent references, too, to the need of facing the cost. "You cannot," Mr. Eden, for instance, told his audience at Edinburgh on May 8, 1942, "run a large Colonial Empire well unless you are determined to do so and proud to make the necessary sacrifices to carry through the task."

Consistent stress has been laid on the evolutionary nature of Great Britain's colonial task. Mr. Macmillan, the Under-Secretary for the Colonies, addressing the House of Commons on June 24, 1942, described the governing principle. It must be, he said, advance from the stage of trusteeship and guardianship to that of equal partnership within the fabric of the Commonwealth; thus, he observed, Great Britain's relation with her Colonies has to be thought of as a permanent, not a transitory, thing. It means, he added, that the Colonial civil services and educational systems must be so organized as to help the people to qualify themselves for administrative posts and, moreover, to want them.

Another point insisted upon in various statements and speeches is the necessity of a greatly intensified effort to improve living standards in poorer Colonies by the sort of means —e.g., the provision of development funds, and setting up of technical research—for which provision was made in the Colonial Development and Welfare Act of 1940, which provides for an expenditure, to be borne by the British taxpayer, of £55,000,000 in the course of ten years.

Finally it is generally recognized that the tempo at which advance towards self-government has up till now proceeded is, in some cases at least, capable of substantial acceleration.

The international facet of British Colonial policy has been brought prominently to the fore by public criticism in the United States. Perhaps the most positive British statement on the international side has been that of Mr. Oliver Stanley, who succeeded Lord Cranborne as Colonial Secretary, when addressing a meeting in Oxford on March 5, 1943. After reaffirming that the administration of the British Colonies must continue to be the sole responsibility of Great Britain, he went on to say: "I myself give no support to a theory, which I think now gains few adherents, that it would be for the benefit of a particular colony or for the benefit of the world as a whole that the colony should be administered by some international body. I can think of nothing which is more likely in practice to break down and less likely to lead to the steady development of the territory concerned. . . .

"But because I believe, and believe strongly, that the administration must remain British and the sovereignty national, it does not mean that I exclude the possibility of close international cooperation. Indeed, under present circumstances I regard such cooperation not only as desirable but essential. . . . Problems of transport, of economics, of health, et cetera, far transcend the boundaries of a particular political unit, and I therefore should welcome the establishment of machinery which enabled such problems to be discussed and to be solved by common efforts."

The speech was criticized somewhat sharply in the organs of the Liberal and Labour parties, and a fortnight later, on March 18th, the Prime Minister was asked in Parliament whether it represented the policy of His Majesty's Government. He replied to the questioner: "Yes, Sir. His Majesty's Government are convinced that the administration of the British Colonies must continue to be the sole responsibility of Great Britain. The policy of His Majesty's Government is to plan for the fullest possible political, economic and social development of the Colonies within the British Empire, and in close collaboration with neighbouring and friendly nations."

International cooperation, as thus envisaged clearly possesses a double character, (a) regional and specific, (b) in relation to some general international organization. Regarding the former, and in relation specifically to the Far East, the concrete suggestions which have so far been advanced from British quarters have been unofficial in character.[3] They were embodied in a

[3] But it may be noted that Mr. Oliver Stanley in a speech recorded in *The Times* of December 22, 1942, referred to the Anglo-American Caribbean Com-

speech delivered by Lord Hailey in Toronto on December 18, 1942, during a tour in Canada after the closing of the I.P.R. Conference. The proposals which Lord Hailey enunciated were for the setting up of Regional Councils representative of the sovereign States having interests in the region in question, and endowed with the functions of advising the Governments concerned on the economic and social advance achieved in each of the dependent areas, and, further, of reviewing periodically the progress which was being made towards self-government and the improvement of living conditions. This, it was considered, would help towards the goal of securing a common policy in economic and social development inside the region as a whole.

On the second and wider plane, cooperation with other Powers in colonial affairs would, as envisaged by British spokesmen, take in the first instance, the form of the building up of a system, or systems, of security. This, it seems to be generally agreed, would be especially needed in the case of the western Pacific. The precedence to be given to the problem of security in all postwar reorganization in the international sphere has been emphasized by more than one British statesman. In the House of Lords on June 4, 1942, Lord Selborne, speaking for the Government, declared the conception of the Atlantic Charter to be that of collective security, "and it is in this direction," he added, "that we are bending our thoughts." Mr. Eden spoke strongly on the subject in his Edinburgh address, quoted above. He said that peace and the guarding of peace was the first preliminary to social advance. For this cause the United Nations must, he considered, possess enough military force after the war to provide for policing, for on them would lie the main burden of sustaining a peace system. Carrying the argument further, he went on to say that force is, of course, not enough; peace will depend, too, on social improvement and will stand in jeopardy so long as wholesale unemployment, malnutrition, or animal standards of life prevail in any part of the world.

Mr. Herbert Morrison, at the Guildhall on February 20, 1943, maintained the same thesis in regard to the responsibility of the four leading United Nations as the power wielding guard-

---

mission's work as an example of the kind of international cooperation in Colonial matters which he hoped to see combined with the continuance of national sovereignty.

ians of peace. The Home Secretary then proceeded to investigate the possibilities of a "representative world political association." Such an association would be necessary, he believed, in order to mobilize the "free consent of free peoples" behind the police functions of the four Powers.

The special application to the Far Eastern region of such principles as these has not, however, yet been officially adumbrated. The documents contributed to the I.P.R. Conference by the United Kingdom delegation and speeches made by its members serve, nevertheless, to show that a feeling exists in responsible British circles that some form of collective security will probably be indispensable in the western Pacific area, and that the need for this must be taken into account in any regional reconstruction planning by the Powers concerned.

The views of the Labour Party in Great Britain have been set out in a report on *Post-war Policy for the African and Pacific Colonies* issued on April 3, 1943. The authors maintain that Colonial territories should be administered primarily as a trust for the native inhabitants. They see advantages in the Crown Colony type of administration as allowing of the gradual transition to responsible government, and they approve also of the system of indirect rule, making use of native institutions, provided that these institutions ensure training in self-government and that they are not used to maintain the autocratic powers of native rulers.

As regards international aspects of the management of colonial territories, the report considers that world peace must be safeguarded by generalizing the strategical and economic advantages of colonial possessions. On the strategical side this could only be brought about by the establishment of a general international system exercising the constant threat and fear of war. As regards the economic side, there should be economic equality for all States in respect of access of raw materials, markets and the field of capital investment in the colonies. This, the report points out, would involve a reversal of the "imperial preference" policy inaugurated by the Ottawa Agreements. There is also a recommendation that the clause in the League of Nations Covenant establishing mandates should be amplified and made to apply to all "backward" colonial territories.

The report is to be submitted for approval to the Labour Party Conference which is due to take place in June of the present year.

APPENDIX I

EXTRACT FROM THE (NINE POWER) TREATY OF WASHINGTON FEBRUARY 6, 1922[1]

Article I: The Contracting Powers, other than China, agree

(1) To respect the sovereignty, the independence, and the territorial and administrative integrity of China;

(2) To provide the fullest and most unembarrassed opportunity to China to develop and maintain for herself an effective and stable Government;

(3) To use their influence for the purpose of effectually establishing and maintaining the principle of equal opportunity for the commerce and industry of all nations throughout the territory of China;

(4) To refrain from taking advantage of conditions in China in order to seek special rights or privileges which would abridge the rights of subjects or citizens of friendly States, and from countenancing action inimical to the security of such States.

[1] British White Paper, Cmd. 1627.

APPENDIX II

EXTRACT FROM BRITISH MEMORANDUM ON CHINA, DECEMBER 18, 1926[2]

... 6. His Majesty's Government, after carefully reviewing the position, desire to submit their considered opinion as to the course which the Washington Treaty Powers should now adopt. His Majesty's Government propose that these Governments shall issue a statement setting forth the essential facts of the situation; declaring their readiness to negotiate on treaty revision and all other outstanding questions as soon as the Chinese themselves have constituted a Government with authority to negotiate; and stating their intention pending the establishment of such a Government to pursue a constructive policy in harmony with the spirit of the Washington Conference but developed and adapted to meet the altered circumstances of the present time.

7. His Majesty's Government propose that in this joint declaration the Powers should make it clear that in their constructive policy they desire to go as far as possible towards meeting the legitimate aspirations of the Chinese nation. They should abandon the idea that the economic and political development of China can only be secured under foreign tutelage, and should declare their readiness to recognize her right to the enjoyment of tariff autonomy as soon as she herself has settled and promulgated a new national tariff. They should expressly disclaim any intention of forcing foreign control upon an unwilling China. While calling upon China to maintain that respect for the sanctity of treaties which is the primary obligation common to all civilized States, the Powers should yet recognize both the essential justice of the Chinese claim for treaty revision and the difficulty under present conditions of negotiating new treaties in place of the old, and they should therefore modify their traditional attitude of rigid insistence on the strict letter of treaty rights. During this possibly very prolonged period of uncertainty the Powers can only, in the view of His Majesty's Government, adopt an expectant attitude and endeavour to shape developments so far as possible in conformity with the realities of the situation so that

[2] Communicated by H. M. Chargé d'Affaires at Peking on December 18, 1926, to the Representatives of the Washington Treaty Powers. *The Times*, December 28, 1926.

ultimately, when treaty revision becomes possible, it will be found that part at least of the revision has already been effected on satisfactory lines. It would therefore be wise to abandon the policy of ineffective protest over minor matters, reserving protest—which should then be made effective by united action—only for cases where vital interests are at stake. Every case should be considered on its merits and the declaration should show that the Powers are prepared to consider in a sympathetic spirit any reasonable proposals that the Chinese authorities, wherever situated, may make, even if contrary to strict interpretation of treaty rights, in return for fair and considerate treatment of foreign interests by them. The declaration should show that it is the policy of the Powers to endeavor to maintain harmonious relations with China without waiting for or insisting on the prior establishment of a strong Central Government.

APPENDIX III

BRITISH NOTE PRESENTED TO JAPAN, JANUARY 14, 1939[3]

"I am instructed by his Majesty's Principal Secretary of State for Foreign Affairs to inform Your Excellency of the uncertainty and the grave anxiety in which His Majesty's Government in the United Kingdom have been left by a study of Japan's new policy in Far Eastern affairs, as set out in recent statements by the late Prime Minister and other Japanese statesmen. I am to refer more particularly to Prince Konoye's statements of November 3 and December 22 and to the communication made by Your Excellency to foreign Press correspondents on December 19. This uncertainty has not been removed by conversations on this subject which I have had with Your Excellency from time to time.

From these pronouncements and from other official information issued in Japan, His Majesty's Government infer that it is the intention of the Japanese Government to establish a tripartite combination or *bloc* composed of Japan, China, and Manchuria, in which the supreme authority will be vested in Japan and subordinate roles will be allotted to China and Manchuria. So far as China is concerned it is understood that the Japanese Government are to exercise control, at least for some time, through the Asia Development Council in Tokyo, which is charged with the formulation and execution of policy connected with political, economic, and cultural affairs in China. Your Excellency's own communication to the Press indicates that the tripartite combination is to form a single economic unit, and the economic activities of other Powers are to be subjected to restrictions dictated by the requirements of national defence and the economic security of the proposed *bloc*.

According to Prince Konoye, the hostilities in China are to continue until the present Chinese Government have been crushed or will consent to enter the proposed combination on Japanese terms. China, he said, will be required to conclude with Japan an anti-Comintern agreement and Japanese troops are to be stationed at specified points in Chinese territory for an indefinite period, presumably to ensure that the Japanese conditions for the suspen-

[3] Handed to the Japanese Foreign Minister by the British Ambassador in Tokyo. *The Times*, January 16, 1939.

sion of hostilities are observed. Moreover, His Excellency stated that the Inner Mongolian region must be designated as a special anti-Communist area. It is not clear what is meant by this, but in the absence of fuller information it can only be assumed that Inner Mongolia is to be subjected to an even greater degree of Japanese military control than other parts of China.

His Majesty's Government are at a loss to understand how Prince Konoye's assurance that Japan seeks no territory, and respects the sovereignty of China, can be reconciled with the declared intentions of the Japanese Government to compel the Chinese people by force of arms to accept conditions involving the surrender of their political, economic, and cultural life to Japanese control, the indefinite maintenance in China of considerable Japanese garrisons, and the virtual detachment from China of the territory of Inner Mongolia.

For their part, His Majesty's Government desire to make it clear that they are not prepared to accept or to recognize changes of the nature indicated, which are brought about by force. They intend to adhere to the principles of the Nine-Power Treaty, and cannot agree to the unilateral modification of its terms. They would point out that, until the outbreak of the present hostilities, the beneficial effects which the Treaty was expected to produce were steadily being realized. The Chinese people were maintaining and developing for themselves an effective and stable Government, and the principle of equal opportunity for the commerce and industry of all nations was bringing prosperity to China and to her international trade, including that with Japan. His Majesty's Government therefore cannot agree, as suggested in Japan, that the Treaty is obsolete or that its provisions no longer meet the situation, except in so far as the situation has been altered by Japan in contravention of its terms.

While, however, His Majesty's Government maintain that modifications cannot be effected unilaterally and must be by negotiation between all the signatories, they do not contend that treaties are eternal. If, therefore, the Japanese Government have any constructive suggestions to make regarding the modification of any of the multilateral agreements relating to China, His Majesty's Government for their part will be ready to consider them. In the meantime, His Majesty's Government reserve all their rights under the existing treaties.

I am further instructed to refer to that portion of Prince Konoye's statement of December 22 which states that Japan is prepared to give consideration to the abolition of extra-territoriality and the rendition of foreign concessions and settlements in China. This inducement to China to accept Japan's demands would appear to entail but little sacrifice on the part of the Japanese, for if they succeed in their plans for the control of the country they will have no further need for extra-territoriality or concessions. On the other hand, His Majesty's Government would recall that they undertook and nearly completed negotiations with the Chinese Government in 1931 for the abrogation of British extra-territorial rights. The negotiations were suspended by the Chinese Government in consequence of the disturbed conditions following seizure of Manchuria by Japanese forces in that year, but His Majesty's Government have always been ready to resume negotiations at a suitable time, and are prepared to discuss this and other similar questions with a fully independent Chinese Government when peace has been restored.

In conclusion, I am to state, that, if, as is possible, His Majesty's Government have in any way misinterpreted the intentions of the Japanese Government, they feel that it is because of the ambiguity with which those intentions have so far been expressed, and they would welcome a more precise and detailed exposition of the Japanese conditions for terminating the hostilities and of the Japanese policy towards China."

INDEX

THE I.P.R. INQUIRY SERIES

At the invitation of the Institute of Pacific Relations, scholars in many countries have been engaged since early in 1938 in the preparation of studies forming part of an Inquiry into the problems arising from the conflict in the Far East. The purpose of this Inquiry is to provide an impartial and constructive analysis of the major issues which may have to be considered in any future adjustment of international relations in that area.

The studies include an account of the economic and political conditions which led to the outbreak of fighting in July 1937, with respect to China, to Japan and to the other foreign Powers concerned; an evaluation of developments during the war period which affect the policies of all the Powers in relation to the Far Eastern situation; and, finally, an estimate of the principal political, economic and social conditions which may be expected in a post-war period, the possible forms of adjustment which might be applied under these conditions, and the effects of such adjustments upon the countries concerned.

The Inquiry does not propose to "document" a specific plan for dealing with the Far Eastern situation. Its aim is to present information in forms which will be useful to those who lack the time or expert knowledge to study the vast amount of material now appearing in a number of languages. A list of Inquiry studies already completed appears on the following pages.

SOME OTHER STUDIES ALREADY COMPLETED IN THE I.P.R. INQUIRY SERIES

JAPANESE INDUSTRY: ITS RECENT DEVELOPMENT AND PRESENT CONDITION, by G. C. Allen, Brunner Professor of Economic Science, University of Liverpool.   124 pages. $1.00

ECONOMIC SHANGHAI: HOSTAGE TO POLITICS, 1937-1941, by Robert W. Barnett, International Secretariat, Institute of Pacific Relations.   210 pages. $2.00

AMERICAN POLICY IN THE FAR EAST, 1931-1941, Revised Edition by T. A. Bisson, Foreign Policy Association. With a supplementary chapter by Miriam S. Farley, American Council, Institute of Pacific Relations.   208 pages. $1.75

GERMAN INTERESTS AND POLICIES IN THE FAR EAST, by Kurt Bloch, American Council, Institute of Pacific Relations.
     75 pages. $1.00

JAPAN SINCE 1931, by Hugh Borton. Assistant Professor of Japanese, Columbia University.   141 pages. $1.25

THE ECONOMIC DEVELOPMENT OF THE NETHERLANDS INDIES, by Jan O. M. Broek, Associate Professor of Geography, University of California.   172 pages. $2.00

GOVERNMENT AND NATIONALISM IN SOUTHEAST ASIA, by Rupert Emerson, Formerly Associate Professor of Government, Harvard University; Lennox A. Mills, Associate Professor of Political Science, University of Minnesota; Virginia Thompson, Research Associate, Institute of Pacific Relations.
     242 pages. $2.00

THE CHINESE ARMY, by Major Evans Fordyce Carlson, United States Marine Corps, Recently Resigned.   139 pages. $1.00

EDUCATIONAL PROGRESS IN SOUTHEAST ASIA, by J. S. Furnewall.   186 pages. $2.00

POST-WAR WORLDS, by P. E. Corbett, Professor of International Law and Chairman of the Social Sciences and Commerce Group, McGill University.   211 pages. $2.00

FAR EASTERN TRADE OF THE UNITED STATES, by Ethel B. Dietrich, Professor of Economics, Mt. Holyoke College.
     116 pages. $1.00

GOVERNMENT IN JAPAN, *by* Charles B. Fahs, Assistant Professor of Oriental Affairs, Pomona and Claremont Colleges.

114 pages. $1.00

THE PROBLEM OF JAPANESE TRADE EXPANSION IN THE POST-WAR SITUATION, *by* Miriam S. Farley, American Council, Institute of Pacific Relations. 93 pages. $1.00

BRITISH RELATIONS WITH CHINA: 1931-1939, *by* Irving S. Friedman, International Secretariat, Institute of Pacific Relations. 256 pages. $2.00

FRENCH INTERESTS AND POLICIES IN THE FAR EAST, *by* Roger Lévy, Chargé de Cours Ecole Nationale de la France d'Outremer; Guy Lacam, Formerly Director of the Economic Department of the Bank of Indo-China; Andrew Roth, International Secretariat, Institute of Pacific Relations.

209 pages. $2.00

CANADA AND THE FAR EAST, 1940, *by* A. R. M. Lower, Professor of History, United College, University of Manitoba.

152 pages. $1.25

NEW ZEALAND'S INTERESTS AND POLICIES IN THE FAR EAST, *by* Ian F. G. Milner, New Zealand Institute for Educational Research. 131 pages. $1.00

INDUSTRIALIZATION OF THE WESTERN PACIFIC, *by* Kate L. Mitchell, Research Associate, Institute of Pacific Relations.

322 pages. $2.50

JAPAN'S EMERGENCE AS A MODERN STATE, *by* E. Herbert Norman, International Secretariat, Institute of Pacific Relations.

254 pages. $2.00

PREREQUISITES TO PEACE IN THE FAR EAST, *by* Nathaniel Peffer, Associate Professor of International Relations, Columbia University. 121 pages. $1.00

AUSTRALIA'S INTERESTS AND POLICIES IN THE FAR EAST, *by* Jack Shepherd, International Secretariat, Institute of Pacific Relations. 212 pages. $2.00

BANKING AND FINANCE IN CHINA, *by* Frank M. Tamagna

400 pages. $4.00

ITALY'S INTERESTS AND POLICIES IN THE FAR EAST, *by* Frank M. Tamagna, Instructor in Economics, Xavier University.

91 pages. $1.00

STRUGGLE FOR NORTH CHINA, *by* George E. Taylor, Assistant Professor of Oriental Studies, University of Washington.

247 pages. $2.00

LEGAL PROBLEMS IN THE FAR EASTERN CONFLICT, *by* Quincy
Wright, Professor of Law, University of Chicago; H. Lauter-
pacht, Professor of International Law, Cambridge University; Edwin M. Borchard, Professor of International Law,
Yale University, and Phoebe Morrison, Research Associate
in International Law, Yale University.   211 pages. $2.00